I0391403

Timeless Writings

31

Tatay Jobo Elizes
Compiler
2017

Published by Tatay Jobo Elizes, Self-Publisher

This book is published and printed under the expressed permission of the various authors compiled for this purpose of making their articles and essays available to the public and promote reading among Filipinos, young and old. Authors own the copyrights to their writings. Authors can withdraw or rescind their permission anytime and will be edited out in next printing. Printing of this book is using the present day method of Print-On-Demand (POD) or Book-On-Demand (BOD) systems, where prints will never run out of copies. Authors are free to republish or reprint with other publishers and printers anytime.

ISBN Codes

ISBN – 13: 978 – 1542695312   and
ISBN – 10: 1542695317

Disclaimer: Views are expressed by the authors alone. Tatay Jobo Elizes does not knowingly publish false information or commit copyright infringement having been given explicit permission to publish this book. Tatay Jobo Elizes may not be held liable for the views of the authors exercising their right to free expression.

Self-Publisher's Details:
Contact: job_elizes@yahoo.com
Websites: http:tinyurl.com/mj76ccq +
www.jobelizes6.wix.com/mysite

Contents

1.

Marjo Letter to Gramma
Marjorie Ann Elizes Reyes
January 11, 2017

My dearest Gramma (and everyone),

As talkative as I am, I have no idea how I'll be doing this letter, so I'm just typing as my thoughts come along.

First thing that I want to tell you is that I am sorry. I'm sorry that we lost Mama. I know that you love her very much. I may not know how you exactly feel because I have no children of my own yet, but I want you to know that I share this feeling of loss with you, and that you are not alone in facing this very difficult road, for we are all with you. It may not always seem like it, with everything you are witnessing at home, but please believe that she is always in our thoughts every second of every day.

It might even be one of the reasons why we're all so messed up right now, because we are very much affected, and have no clue in dealing with it, so we deal with it in different ways, and has not resulted well for this family.. It is very difficult to accept because none of us were ready giving her up yet, everything will be different for us, occasions, gatherings, restaurants we go to, shopping time, skype time, everything.

Even just the feel of this house is so different, there will always be that empty spot. There will always be that question WHY. Why her? Why now?

Why? And what's worse is that we can't even get an answer for that question....yet. We have all these questions and honestly might even feel angry with how things turn out in our lives.

But what I learned while I am constantly building and improving my relationship with our dear God is that, everything, EVERYTHING will always have a purpose. Things may not be how we want them to be, we may get things now, and have some things late, or even denied. But all of that is just in His time, and His will. For He will always have the best plan for us, and would always be bigger and better than what we have planned for ourselves. And it would always be for our own good. So I guess what I am trying to say is, which I know will always be easier said than done, but this is God's plan for us, and we should or at least try our best to find it in our hearts to accept that, and just take it day by day as it goes, and trust Him that He needed to bring Mama back to His kingdom because that is the best for her, and the time lent and purpose given to her here with us is done already.

But that would never mean that we would stop thinking about her, or missing her, or loving her. We just have to keep her most alive now in our hearts, where all of our memories of her will be stored and cherished for the rest of our lives.

I also want to say thank you. I couldn't even decide on what to put first with all the things I am thankful for. If there's one thing I am thankful for that can sum it all up is that I want to thank you for being there. Honestly I can't even imagine this if you all were not there. I remember the day I told Mama you guys were confirming on flying here. I saw the purest joy and hope in her face, and I know that it gave her more strength to just keep on fighting, because you all were there also rooting for her, and fighting with her. Given the tremendous distance apart, you all closed that gap and gave her that assurance of love and support. That is something that would always be different from what we can give her, so thank you. In part with that, I am very grateful for the care you all are giving us. Thank you for the concern, and the support as well.

I wish you all could have stayed longer, thank you for letting gramma maximize her stay here. It may not seem like it sometimes, but I really really REALLY appreciate your stay here with us gramma. I really do. Thank you na sinamahan niyo po kami for a while. And now as you fly back to Brooklyn, I'm scared. I'm so scared because this is really the "back to reality" part where it's just the four of us, that used to be five. This is so overwhelming I don't even know where to start. I feel pressured, tired, scared, challenged, insecure, I just don't know how to pick up the pieces and how to start again. And the thought of starting again with Mama not here is what hurts the most. I want to fix all the issues and broken pieces we have, I want to take care of this family and make it stronger and solid, but it would always require a group effort, and that's what I am praying for right now. Can I ask that you guys always pray with me too, that even in the darkest of times and in the times we feel most destroyed, may we always remember that we still have each other, and we should not take that for granted. May love, peace, and forgiveness always dwell in our family, and may God always be the center of everything. For we can always do things through Christ who strengthens us.

I'm not good with sayings or cliche lines, but

I've heard once or twice that in loss, you also gain. Nothing will ever be on level with losing Mama, but if there's something that I want us to gain from this loss, is that we gain more and more love and patience for one another, and may her death be a reminder of how capable we are of being strong, when we never really knew how strong we were when being strong was the only choice we had, and how being strong for one another gave us the opportunity to reconnect, and to fight this battle with Mama until the very end.

I, for sure, have no idea what's ahead of us. But I just know, that wherever we choose to go, as long as we pray, God will always guide us to the right path. And Mama will be watching beside Him. ©

I love you all. And I pray we can all reunite again, but this time being able to remember and talk about Mama with smiles and laughter on our faces, and nothing but peace and love in our hearts.

Missing you already, Gramma. Praying for your health, and everyone's as well.

You all take care always, and hope to see you all soon.

Love,
Marjo

2.

Are Duterte and Trump the new normal?

November 18, 2016
| Featured, Opinion, PerryScope

PerryScope
By Perry Diaz

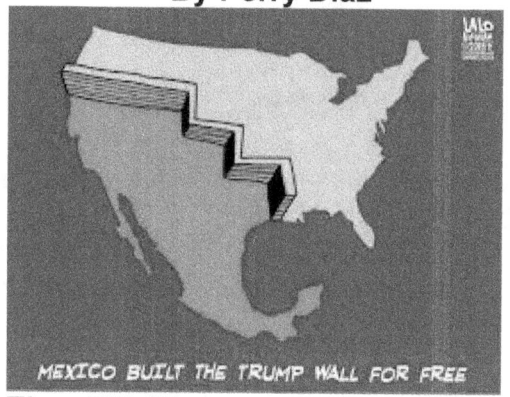

MEXICO BUILT THE TRUMP WALL FOR FREE

The "Wall" at the U.S.-Mexico border proposed by Trump.

The election of Rodrigo R. Duterte and Donald J. Trump — six months apart – as president of the Philippines and United States, respectively, shook the world in a manner that differed from previous presidential elections in both countries. While Duterte was favored to win in large part due to his promise to kill drug pushers and users, Trump was doomed to lose simply because of his controversial stand against a lot of issues and causes that many people consider as "sacred cows." But as it turned out, the "sacred cows" were as fair game as anything else, which — surprisingly

– had attracted the support of many Americans. "I'll build the wall and tell Mexico to pay for it," Trump promised, and his supporters went a-gaga!

It's the same thing with Duterte who told his supporters at a campaign rally: "I'll kill 100,000 drug pushers and users and throw their bodies into the Manila Bay to fatten the fishes." And his supporters went bananas!

Yes, it's indeed a world gone crazy! What the hell happened? But the question should be: "What happened in hell?" And hell is what *hoi polloi* think of the environment they're living in today, which reminds me of Dan Brown's book, *"Inferno."* A character, *Dr. Brooks,* who was visiting Manila said, *"I've run through the gates of hell,"* to describe the crime, poverty, and sex trade that she saw.

And for all the hellish situations that the people have to coup with, they can only blame their governments for not doing enough to make their lives worth living. And all the politicians running for office in both countries – two of the freest democracies on earth – know it. Duterte and Trump saw an opportunity to get ahead of the crowded pack of presidential wannabes by inflaming the emotions of the people. While some people laughed them off, a growing number of people began to wonder, "Why not?"

Duterte made "War on Drugs" the cornerstone of his campaign for the presidency. And true enough he delivered. During his first 100 days in office, more than 4,000 drug pushers and users ended up dead on the streets. The police said that the police gunned down 1,200 of them when they resisted arrest. The rest were tagged as "death under investigation" (DUI), a newly coined term for someone killed under mysterious circumstances, mostly by vigilantes.

"Build the wall"

Meanwhile, as Trump savored his stunning victory over Hillary Clinton who won the popular vote — which doesn't count — but lost the electoral vote to Trump, a lot of Americans wonder how Trump would craft his domestic programs and foreign policy, after all those nasty things that he said about certain groups of Americans and America's allies as well.

If there is one scorching issue that has ignited emotional backlash from Trump's supporters, it's "illegal immigration." With an estimated 11 million illegals residing in the U.S., Trump's solution to this problem is two-fold. First, deport the illegals. And second, build a wall to prevent them from entering the U.S. by way of the porous U.S.-Mexico border. Then he inflamed his supporters' emotion when he accused the Mexican government of sending criminals, rapists, drug pushers, and other undesirable across the border. He promised that the Mexican government would pay for the wall's construction. The question is: Is Mexico willing to pay for the wall?

But regardless of whether Mexico would pay for the wall or not, the perceived "danger" of undesirable aliens crossing the border in record numbers has already been ingrained in the minds of his supporters. In other words, Trump stoked xenophobic fear of Mexican illegal immigrants, which he considers as a threat to national security.

Geopolitics is addition

Duterte, Xi, Putin: The new triumvirate?

If there is one major and critical area of concern among geopolitical experts, it's foreign policy. Duterte made headlines during his state visit to China last October when he declared that he was pursuing an "independent foreign policy." He also announced his "separation" from the U.S., which caused a geopolitical tremor of tectonic proportion, which left the Philippines' allies — particularly the U.S. – trembling. And to drive his point, he said that he would seek economic and military alliance with China and Russia.

Duterte's flirting with China and Russia is nothing more than "puppy love." But what truly caused a lot of headaches among America's allies were Trump's threats to withdraw American forces from Japan and South Korea unless they pay the cost of their deployment in their countries. He also made similar threats to America's NATO allies and even suggested that NATO disbands, which made Russian President Vladimir Putin happier than Dr. Strangelove fiddling with the Doomsday Machine.

But in the event that Duterte and Trump find solace to the notion that foreign policy is not zero-sum game but an intricate art of "geopolitics is addition," they just might play down their rhetoric and do what is best for their people. Let me put it this way: Duterte will need America more than China and Russia combined, while Trump needs NATO as a counterforce to Russian expansion. He also needs America's treaty allies Japan, South Korea, Australia, Philippines, Thailand, and Taiwan to contain China and North Korea.

But there is a silver lining to all the gloom and doom that Trump has been trumpeting around; he wants to make the U.S. stronger to maintain the balance of power in a world in turmoil. During the final days of this year's presidential elections, Trump laid out an ambitious plan to build 350 new warships for the U.S. Navy to match the growing navies of China and Russia.

Ideological shift

Who will Trump nominate to take the late Justice Antonin Scalia's seat?

But the most significant aspect of Duterte and Trump's elections is that both of them will have the opportunity to change the ideological make-up of their respective country's Supreme Court. In the case of Duterte, he'd be appointing 11 new Supreme Court Justices to replace justices who will be retiring when they reach the mandatory retirement age of 70. With only four justices left from the current bench, Duterte – who is an avowed leftist – would presumably appoint justices in his own image.

In the case of the U.S. Supreme Court where there is no mandatory retirement age, Trump will surely nominate a hard-core conservative to take the seat of the late ultra-conservative Justice Antonin Scalia; thus, maintaining the conservative majority on the High Court. However, Justice Anthony Kennedy, although considered a conservative, had oftentimes held the swing vote in big cases; thus, giving the liberals a tactical edge over the conservatives. Another swing vote is Chief Justice John Roberts, who wrote the majority opinion in favor of Obamacare to the chagrin of his fellow conservatives.

However, the shaky equilibrium on the High Court might tilt to the conservative side if one or two of the four liberals' seats were vacated. Among the conservatives, Justice Kennedy at 80 is the oldest. If his seat is vacated, Trump would nominate an ideological conservative to take his seat; thus, solidly strengthening the conservative bloc on the Supreme Court.

With Duterte exiting in six years and Trump in four or eight years, both would leave a lasting legacy that would determine the future of their respective countries. Duterte would leave a left-leaning Supreme Court while Trump would leave the most conservative Supreme Court for the last 50 years, if not the last century.

At the end of the day, what we're seeing is that unorthodoxy has become an acceptable behavior among our political leaders. Duterte and Trump's campaign styles have led people to call Duterte the Trump of the Philippines and Trump as the Duterte of the U.S. Their opponents have called them "loose cannons." But loose cannons or not, they're now the leaders of their countries, which begs the question: Are Duterte and Trump the new normal?

3.

Christmas Day is for Children
Fr Shay Cullen, mssc
23 December 2016

I am standing in the center of the spacious main hall, the atrium, of the new Preda children's home for girls. The light from the transparent roof throws its soft and gentle light on the children playing nosily, shouting in glee. They are happy, running about, playing games, and laughing, cheerful and joyful. They had a sumptuous Christmas dinner and gifts and new clothes. They are the lucky ones to have found refuge and protection and a chance to start their childhood over. Soon they will go on trips to the zoo and then to the fun park and other Christmas treats will come their way. There will be Christmas mass and joyful singing and some will have sad memories of childhood before coming to Preda.

Maggie is only 14 years old and I see her chasing Elizabeth, they are enjoying the fun. Later they will go to their sports and karate. She is gaining weight in the recent weeks as she eats three times a day with snacks in between. She sleeps in a comfortable bed and has her personal things close to her, a doll to cuddle and friends to listen to her as she tells about her life.

When she first came into the Preda home for girls, Margie was quiet, withdrawn and fearful of what she would find. However the welcome and introduction to the other children and their embrace said they would be her friends. This gave her courage and a smile and her nervousness evaporated. Soon she felt at home, accepted and welcome. This was a place where she was safe from her abusers and free from fear and the control of her human traffickers. This was a happy place where the girls choose on their own free will to stay and find education, affirmation and empowerment through therapy, counseling and education.

Christmas has it joys but there are also the sorrows of life .The poverty and neglect suffered by the Holy Family is one of them. They were rejected at the Inn and Mary had to give birth in a dirty animal pen. In humiliating and poverty-stricken circumstances Jesus of Nazareth came into this world. Then we cannot forget the death threats and flight from the evil murderer King Herod who was committing genocide against the innocent children slaughtering hundreds. The impoverished life as a refugee in a foreign country was how he spent the first years of his life.

Maggie was a slim, malnourished and undersized child when she first came into the Preda girls home a few months ago. She was traumatized and has had a terrible experience. Her mother worked for a powerful man. During her employment and afterwards, it appears he sexually abused the child and brought her to various other men in hotels around San Fernando, Pampanga. These men sexually abused her also on twenty occasions. The Preda paralegal officer filed the formal complaint against the suspect. It is feared that the mother of Maggie was approving or allowed the abuse to happen. She may have received money to let it happen.

And it's only one of hundreds of thousands of children like Maggie in the world and especially in the Philippines where there is a massacre of the youth in a campaign against the use of illegal drugs. The latest report by Unicef and the Philippine Council for the Welfare of Children in the report named, National Baseline Study on Violence against Children (NBS-VAC), tells us the horror and extent of the abuse: Eight of 10 Filipino youth suffer abuse: verbal, physical or sexual. Young children and youth between 13-24 years of age, one in every five is a victim of sexual abuse, most of it happening in their homes.

So while we campaign and work to bring Christ into Christmas and save the children, we are unheard because of the futility to persuade government to care for the children to protect them and heal them. We campaign to persuade the moral majority to demand the cancellation of mayor's permits and close the sex bars and clubs. We appeal to Church people to speak out.

In these dens of iniquity where foreign sex tourists proliferate, youth and children are sexually abused daily. Many are subjected to forced drug use and abortions. Like Maggie, they are helpless victims of exploitation and the threats of powerful adults.

Many corrupt government officials, senators and representatives are morally bankrupt and ignore the plight and suffering of the innocents. They want the death penalty and to make 9 year old children suffer as criminals. We need a strong outspoken and uncompromising leader to bring about a moral revolution in society. Yet none has the courage to emerge.

Christmas is happy and joyful for those saved and healed but so much has to be done to save the thousands more. That moral revolution to protect children's rights, bring compassion and care back again is just a dream. It was brought into this world by the birth of Jesus of Nazareth but it has long been forgotten. All we have left is jingle bells.

We who still believe in the values that make us compassionate and decent loving humans must take our stand and work to bring about that spiritual revolution of mind and heart that will change the world.

- *Need Help? Contact: newsletters@preda.org*
- *Privacy Policy:*
We will never share, sell, or rent individual personal information with anyone without your advance permission or unless ordered by a court of law. Information submitted to us is only available to employees managing this information for purposes of contacting you or sending you emails based on your request for information and to contracted service providers for purposes of providing services relating to our communications with you.
- *Physical Address:*
CONTACT US:
PREDA Foundation, Inc.
P.O Box 68
Olongapo City 2200
Preda Main Center
Upper Kalaklan, Subic Bay
Olongapo City 2200 Philippines
E-mail: shaycullen@preda.org, Information Officer: predainfo@preda.org
TO SUPPORT THE WORK OF PREDA you may freely pass on the article or republish and send a donation via mail or PAYPAL at our website http://www.preda.org or through the Columban Missionary Society.

---ooo---

4.

MEDJUGORIE, HERE THEY COME
Fred Natividad

Dateline, 1995

For some years some Franciscan priests had been promoting the story of the Virgin Mary appearing as an apparition to some children in a mountain town called Medjugorie in what was then Yugoslavia. To a cynical unbeliever the story is a blatant recycling of the story of a girl named Bernadette in Lourdes France. Pilgrimages to Medjugorie has become an exercise in keeping up with the Joneses, especially to some Filipinos in the Chicago area.

One dreary evening some Filipinos were at O'hare on their way to Medjugorie.

The women chatted noisily at the international terminal at O'hare airport. To non-Filipinos they sounded talking in some kind of pidgin notoriously common in the Philippines as Taglish. It is a murderous mixture of Tagalog and English.

Actually nobody really paid much attention to the chattering group except a few white ladies, beyond middle age, who did corner-of-the-eye glances. They may have been from some hick town where they have never seen nor heard chatty Filipino women, or they were just nosy characters accumulating some gossip to tell their neighbors over the fence back home.

Chicago, for one thing, is full of immigrants. And since O'hare is an international airport the sounds of all kinds of strange languages is not unusual. To mainstream Americans Taglish is no more unusual than Swahili. Unless they are trained CIA linguists, the gossip-over-the-fence women can't understand strange tongues anyway.

"Ay, comari, sorprays! Yo ar heyer, olso?"

"Aba, op kors! Si maring Chuchi ay nag-tor na sa Lordis kaya tayo naman sa Mediogori."

"Siyempre!

"Pero, mari, magsa-sayd trip yata tayo sa Pompi..."

"Pompi? Sa Itali yon, ah."

"O-o. Magsi-siyaping tayo ng pornityior."

"Okey, huwag lang nating kalimutang bumile ng stetiyo ni Mama Mary sa Mediogori.

"Di ba marami ka na niyan?"

"O-o, bat alam mo namang wala pang Berhing Mediogori si Chuchi."

"Ay si. Okey, bat witiminit, awt op di wey ang Itali."

"Hmm, yo ar rayt. Okey, magtotor nalang tayo neks yir sa Roma. Malapit ang Pompi doon."

"Eniwey, kabibili lang ni Chuchi ng pornityior sa Marshall Field. Med in Spain daw."

"Ibig sabihin wala pa siyang pornityor na med in Pompi."

Meanwhile, as weather was terrible the Yugoslavian plane that was to take the Chicago pilgrims to Zagreb was delayed in New York. Every minute of delay meant an opportunity for another round of drinks at the bar of the international terminal where half of the customers were husbands of the religious women speaking funny Taglish. The men themselves also bantered in Taglish.

"Pari," one of the men said to another man, "ikaw ba'y bilib sa mirakol sa Mediogori?"

"Noo wiy!"

"Eh, bakit nandito ka?"

"Hino-hyumor ka lang ang misis ko."

"Beri relidiyos ba siya?

"E, marami siyang estetio ng berhin sa bahay, e di relidiyos siya."

"Witi-minit, asawa mo hindi ka syior?"

"Pari, lasing na rin kitang dalawa, ay tenk okey lang to til yo di trot.

"Trot?"

"Gelprin ko lang yan, pari."

"Oki, sa mga panahanon ngayon hindi na yan eskandalos."

"Pari, huwag ka lang maingay. Ang hosban niyan nasa Maynila. Ako naman, ang misis kong nars ay bising nagdo-dobol dyioti gabi-gabi. Si tenks nasa awt-op-tawn bisnis trip ako."

"Tang-na pare, bilib ako sa yo. Por yor abilidad, sa akin ang neks rawn."

"Hindi pari. Sa akin pa rin ang rawn na ito. Pera ng gelprin ko lang naman ang nasa walit ko, e. Anader rawn plis, bartindir..."

The bartindir -er, bartender, gave the two semi-drunk men a cold look, who, he gathered, were on their way to a religious pilgrimage. But, with a forced frozen smile, he poured another round of Scotch for each. He may not like like these little brown hypocrites but he is not stupid - he liked their generous tips.

Just then the public address system blared that the Yugoslavian plane that will take the pilgrims to Zagreb just landed after a two-hour delay in New York. Flight number so-and-so will board in forty-five minutes.The semi-inebriated, nattily dressed brown men gulped their unfinished drinks, paid for their drinks, left generous tips, and went out of the bar to join their forever-chatting ladies.

The bartender watched them with relief because the other casually dressed blue-eyed customers began to grimace each time a Filipino in a suit and tie said something loudly in some kind of pidgin. But the bartender was ambivalent - the brown men were good tippers. He has to like them, at least pretend so. They might be coming back to his bar on their way to another trip out of the country.

The group eventually filed into the plane as noisily as when they were waiting at the terminal. As soon as all were seated with seat belts fastened a Filipino priest, their spiritual leader whose travel was fully paid for by the pilgrims, (lucky fellow) promptly began to lead the rosary aloud. He ignored the stewardess who was trying to demonstrate, without enthusiasm, for a hundred million times, the intricacies of surviving a crash, gesturing like a French mime with an orange inflatable vest.

Women from sixteen Filipino couples hastily put out their rosaries and began to respond to the priest. The flight hostess ignored the rosary-clutching women and continued her mime with bored disinterest. She didn't seem bothered at all by the monotonous drone of Hail Mary's.

"Psst," one woman whispered to another between the Holy Mary's, "whir did yo git yor rosary? Ang akin binili ko sa Patima... holi-meri ... mudder-op-gad..."

"Pram Roma ang akin. Pero meron akong med op gold na iniwan ko sa bahay. Galing naman sa Nevers iyon... mudder-op-gad ... pri-poras..."

The men, meanwhile, promptly went to sleep, dreaming of the hour when the flight hostesses with frozen smiles will begin to serve alcoholic drinks. In less than ten hours the pilgrims will land at Zagreb and will be whisked by bus to Dubrovnik and thence to Medjugorie.

Medjugorean merchants, ready with all kinds of rosaries and pictures of the Lady of Medjugorie, will rub their palms in glee to welcome these new suckers. The pilgrims from Chicago will be equally ready. They will giddily unload their precious hard currency into the Medjugorean economy.

And, yes, they will also kneel with reverence at every spot where the tourist guide claimed the Lady of Medjugorie "miraculously" appeared to some village kids. Some of the men will just stay at the hotel to enjoy cold drinks at the bar.

Fred Natividad Posting from historic Virginia   =Say nanlapuan lingawen pian antay arapen. =Alamin ang pinang-galingan upang malaman ang paro-roonan. =Know where we had been to guide us where we are going.

---oOo---

5.

The Challenges of 2017
Father Shay Cullen
December 28, 2016

This coming 2017 will be a momentous year for the political and moral landscape of the planet. There is a rising tide of political and moral challenges facing humanity. Pope Francis will continue his historic reforms of the Church and the Curia, bringing back the Gospel values and true evangelization. He will continue challenging the world to work and cooperate for peace, justice and freedom. He will promote daily the Gospel message of truth, honesty, compassion, mercy and the spirit and values of human rights and the dignity of every individual and community.

The American president Donald Trump and his extreme right wing views are contradicting the liberal, compassionate and more diplomatic approach of President Barak Obama. The New Year will likely be dominated by controversial issues. After Donald Trump takes office on January 20, 2017 a strict immigration policy will be implemented. It will have a huge impact on undocumented residents of the United States affecting all nationalities- Mexicans, Filipinos, Irish and British, just to mention a few who are in the United States undocumented.

Trump will slow the inflow of immigrants and stop accepting refugees. He will accelerate the deportation of all those without legal documentation to be in the USA. This will cause the break up of families, separating children who are citizens from their parents and relatives who are not legal immigrants. Human suffering will follow.

The change in immigration policy to restrict Mexican and South American workers coming legally and many illegally to the United States seasonally for harvesting fruits and vegetables and doing the dirty work will damage the incomes of American farmers and construction companies that rely on the abundant cheap Mexican labor from over the border.

Filipinos will find it harder to get a tourist visa or any kind of visa to visit friends and relatives in the United States. This is because of the change of foreign policy of Philippine President Rodrigo Dutere away from the United States in favor of China and Russia. The requirement of the US immigration not to have supported in any form whatsoever the extrajudicial killings will challenge visa applicants.

This may upset a lot of Filipinos. The US immigration department is becoming strict on the screening of Filipinos especially those who are applying for a visa whether they are in the Philippines or any other country. If a visa applicant has expressed online, on Facebook or any other social media or is known to have supported the extrajudicial killing under the Duterte administration, they will have to comply with the requirements the Torture Victims Protection Act.

On the application form DS-160, they will be asked if they have ever "vommitted, ordered, incited, assisted or otherwise participated in acts of torture. . . or extrajudicial killings as defined in the Torture Victims Protection Act." If the applicant has ever cheered or attended rallies supporting the acts of killing of suspects the applicant has to answer yes. The visa will be likely refused.

If the applicant answers no and it is reported or otherwise comes to light that the applicant did express support for the extrajudicial killings, they could be arrested in the United States and charged with a violation and jailed or deported. It's a serious offense to give false information to the US immigration officials. Under President Trump, it will be strictly enforced.

2017 could be the start of four years of contentious issues. Even if Trump backs away from his more outlandish and provocative campaign rhetoric yet his threats to withdraw from treaties like the Paris climate change agreement will also dominate the New Year.

As the global warming continues to heat up, the message of Pope Francis on the world environment is of greatest importance. The Arctic ice melting quickly, the rising levels of the ocean inundating low-lying islands and coastal towns and villages will cause social unrest globally. There will be outrage and great civil unrest in the United States also as the Trump administration activates the coal industry, leaves basic wages the same, reduces corporate tax to 15 percent and removes protective environmental and financial regulations. The billionaires in his government and outside it will continue their self-enrichment and he will fail to deliver the prosperity promised to the marginalized electorate who voted him into office.

The poor in America and the world will likely realize after a few years of Trump that billionaires do not approve of long term investment for poor communities. They are against development aid for countries of the developing world. They will exploit the poor countries to get a big profit from controlling the raw materials and natural resources. They are there in office not to serve but to enrich their own wealth and that of their companies. If international trade deals are rescinded, it will hurt the US economy as well as many other countries and the poor most of all.

For all of us, 2017 is a challenge with the rise of the right political groups that advocate exclusion and nationalism. This will be countered by the awaking of the broader population to its dangers to democracy yet it will take a few years for it to fade from the political scene as the refugee challenge continues.

We hope and pray for 2017 to see the strengthening of the dignity of the people, an end to the killing of suspects, the reign of justice and peace and respect for the rights of children.

shaycullen@preda.org

- ***Need Help? Contact:***
newsletters@preda.org
- ***Physical Address:***
CONTACT US:
PREDA Foundation, Inc.
P.O Box 68
Olongapo City 2200
Preda Main Center
Upper Kalaklan, Subic Bay
Olongapo City 2200 Philippines
E-mail: shaycullen@preda.org, Information
Officer: predainfo@preda.org
TO SUPPORT THE WORK OF PREDA you may freely pass on the article or republish and send a donation via mail or PAYPAL at our website http://www.preda.org or through the Columban Missionary Society.

---ooo---

6.

Hate and Justice

Jonathan Edwards J. Olabre

Hate and Justice

I was an elementary school student then and after doing my homework and dinner, I would go to my grandfather and watch him stack his books and Bible on the dining table. To the smell of katol, he would read and write to compose his Sunday sermon at church. It took him a few nights to draft, revise and finish his sermon. Sermons at Protestant Sunday Services would last at least an hour back then. Now they just want it short and sweet. But I digress. I would ask so many questions ranging from English subjects, mathematics, science, news that I read on the newspapers all the way to the American era that he grew up in. I would ask what they did since there was no electricity, the games they played and his playmates.

He told me of a playmate, a girl, his neighbor whose parents were Chinese. He told me of how pretty she was and how they were close friends. Tatay (that was how we called our grandfather) did not yet have his brother, Tiyo Bayani as a playmate. They were born 9 years apart. So this girl was his only playmate. Being children that they were, they often would lose track of time while playing. As in such cases, the father of the girl would get angry and punish the girl. Tatay told me how every time it happened she was beaten with a cane. Tatay would tell me how he heard every whoosh of the cane before it struck his playmate on the back, buttocks and legs. The girl never cried out according to Tatay. Tatay would feel the guilt of having been at fault because he felt guilty for playing so late in the day with the girl. Tatay would sit by the window and clench his fists and tremble for every whoosh he would hear. With this story unfolding before me, I also felt anger and rage. I could see his impassive face while he was telling me the story. He told me that his father, my great grandfather, Lolo Pedrito (or Pedrong Paos) to the neighbors, would just put both his hands on Tatay's shoulders to steady him. Lolo Pedrito will not say anything. Just firm hands on Tatay's shoulders. I asked Tatay what it was like to be a witness to such cruelty, to such punishment for so small an infraction? He just told me that he always found his playmate cheerful the next day and then they would play as if nothing had happened the night before. I asked if he was angry and he told me yes he was angry but what surprised me was that he did not have any hate for the father. Tatay told me that the hands on his shoulders were there to steady him, to show that there are things that happen in the world that we cannot control but must have the courage to face no matter how bad it seems. That was why he would play again the next day with his neighbor. He told me he always paid due courtesy to the parents of his playmate. One time, Lolo Pedrito told him "maaaring magalit ngunit walang pagka-muhi.". It is alright to feel anger but never hate. It was the same lesson that my grandfather told me although indirectly that night. Tatay lived on to survive WWII (almost executed by the Japanese on suspicions of being a guerilla) and the tumultuous years of Martial Law. I found him always taking on principled stands with regards to Martial Law. He was old by then but never lot the resolve for talking and discussing what is right and wrong to the chagrin of my uncle who was close to President Marcos.

Why do I tell this? This is why. I came across a column of Contreras that is trying to revise history just for the sake of being "fair" and that history of the Martial Law regime was based on "Hatred". With the death of 5 victims of EJK a block from where I live, I decided to fight back against this Cult of Death and Tyranny being espoused by this professor and columnist.

I will answer it point by point. Italics will be my riposte.

Contreras stated:

IT is wrong to deny the existence of the innocent casualties of martial law.

But it is equally wrong to treat as innocent victims those who by choice took up arms and embraced the communist ideology. They are rebels with a cause, and are in fact freedom fighters. To label them innocent victims is to insult the virtue and the power of their politics.

I say:

Those who took up arms against the dictatorship never professed innocence in the middle of a firefight. It was never heard in the middle of the battle that troops should stop firing since the NPAs were "innocents". I challenge that any after action report be submitted that there were such things. In the event of GRP victories, I have yet to come to read such a report. In cases of NPA victories, there was nary a remark of such tactics.

But I point out to documented evidence that is now at the Human Rights Victims Claims Board that no combatans filed for compensation because they were killed or injured in a firefight. In fact, those huge piles of documents told of imprisonment, torture and death not from firefights.

Contreras says:

These were young students who saw hope in the leftist ideology, urban workers who were politicized by the exploitative working conditions that their capitalist masters inflicted on them, and rural peasants who were in search of liberation from bondage by their oppressive landlords. Their politics is one driven by a revolutionary struggle, and one that they deliberately chose.

I say:

Students who saw hope in leftist ideology? Edgar Jopson was laughed at by the more radical students who belonged to the Kabataang Makabayan (KM) since he was a burgis and malabnaw. He was never a member of KM but of the moderate National Union of Students of the Philippines (NUSP). In fact he was from the Ateneo then, one of two most elitist schools in the Philippines, the other one was De Lasalle College. The other fact is that Marcos himself considered the NUSP as moderate in its stances that he even acceded to an audience with the NUSP leaders. When Edgar Jopson asked that Marcos put in writing that he will not run or aspire for a for a third term (the 1935 Constitution barred any president from a third term), Marcos was livid and remarked "why should I treat with the son of a grocer?" and "why should I listen to them, their English is not even elegant." With such treatment and by declaring Martial Law, I know asked who put the students towards the fold of the only alternative left at that time? When Martial Law was declared, these students and their leaders were rounded up and those who managed to escape the dragnet were driven to the only remaining alternative remaining. Congress was padlocked, The Supreme Court were composed of 9 Marcos appointees out of eleven and the Press was muzzled. What would you have those students do? Join the Mickey Mouse Club?

The workers? Most industries were then controlled by the oligarchy. But then, Marcos was funded in the 1965 Elections by the oligarchy. In fact, the Lopez business empire funded Marcos against Macapagal. The 1969 elections were also funded by the oligarchy. So, who was in any position to stand up for the workers? Philippine industry was in the stranglehold of US business interests at that time. Who else would have the capacity for manufacturing and even agriculture after WWII? Ever heard of Parity Rights? The Laurel-Langley Act gave a sunset provision on it that it would end in 1973. But Marcos using Martial Law extended it for another year. Marcos used the excuse that nationalist economic policies were being espoused by the demonstrators so as that why he also declared Martial Law. This Marcos told to US Ambassador Byroad.

Filipino workers were exploited to the hilt. In fact there was no 60/40 Filipino/Foreigner limit that time. Even in the early 80s, Filipino workers in Mattel, Parke-Davis and Stanford Microsystems were subject to oppression from management and further oppression from the apparatus of Martial Law when it came to fighting for their rights and better compensation. Their leaders were arrested and their picketlines were assaulted and dispersed.

Marcos boasted to potential investors that strikes were prohibited because of Martial Law. If you were a worker then, were would you come to for redress? Marcos drove labor to the left.

Farmers? The 40 days and nights of rain in 1970 brought out the worst flooding in Central Luzon for decades. Central Luzon was considered the Rice Granary of the country. This resulted in rice shortages that extended all the way to 1973. So those who say that the country was self-sufficient in rice during the time of Marcos are on Fentanyl. The only time was in 1977 when there was a chance to export rice but not in big volumes.

The floods during that time so affected the rice farmers. During the flood itself many were just on rooftops while the only idea of Disaster Risk Reduction and Management was footages of the First Lady throwing plastic bags of Nutribuns from Huey Helicopters to families on rooftops. It never occurred that drinking water was also needed. The devastation was so wide that months after the floods, relief and rehabilitation was being conducted. Students from Manila went to the countryside to help in the effort. That was when the students saw the deplorable conditions of the farmers flood or no flood. These students experienced what it was to be a farmer, they told their immersion to fellow students. That was another factor for the rise of student activism. Students saw with their own eyes that there was a malaise. The farmers have nobody and nowhere to turn to. Aside from the generations old tenancies they have no assistance from government.

Declaring Land Reform in 1973 did not solve the problems. The law had conditions that enabled big land holders to retain their landholdings. Why?

Marcos was still of the mind that Martial Law was still unstable and that he needed the support of large landlords or else they would gang up on him if he defied them. The farmers had nobody to turn to. Guess who drove them to the arms NPA?

From a strength of 800 at the declaration Martial Law in 1972, the NPA had at its peak at 26,000 by 1986 before Marcos fled.

Contreras said:

However, theirs are only some of the many political narratives that populated the Marcos years.

There is also the narrative of the state, as an institution that has a right to protect itself from any threat, and in fact has the monopoly of the legitimate use of political violence, only restrained by its commitment to civilized rules of engagement. The burden was for the state to justify its use of violence in accordance with the law. Declaring martial law suspends some rights, but it does not give the state the freedom to kill without justification. Even in war there are rules.

I say:

What were the reasons for Martial Law? What justified it? If we go by the reasons of Marcos such as the NPAs, lawlessness, economic collapse and social decadence, then I answer initially not from a subjective point of view but from a documented source that has institutional credibility until this very day.

There was nothing in the Philippine situation that would have generated panic or hysteria. Just a year before the imposition of martial law, the prestigious Rand Corporation surveyed the Philippine situation on commission from the U.S. Agency for International Development. The Rand report underscored among others the fact that:

1. "The political system appears to be stable and generally responsive to the desire of most people."

2. "The economy appears to be performing better than commonly thought and is spread broadly across the country."

3. "Crime is not a national problem. Violence and fear of violence are concentrated in a few areas."

4. "The HMB (Hukbong Mapagpalaya ng Bayan or NPA) are not a serious threat to the government."

So what in the name of Sam Hill would Marcos declare Martial Law for when even the most Rightist and Conservative Think Tank at that time said there were no reasons to do so?

My gin is almost consumed. I will continue with this tomorrow.

Bilog lang pala katapat mo Contreras!

Hate and Justice Part II
As for Rights that some were only suspended and not all, I beg to differ since freedom and liberty are all the most fundamental of Rights. The fact that the Supreme Court that encompasses the Judiciary was itself defanged:

"I do hereby (further) order that the Judiciary shall continue to function in accordance with its present organization and personnel, and shall try and decide in accordance with existing laws all criminal and civil cases, except the following :

1. Those involving the validity, legality or constitutionality of Proclamation No. 1081, dated September 21,1972, or of any decree, order or acts issued, promulgated or performed by me or by my duly designated representative pursuant thereto.

2. Those involving the validity, legality or constitutionality of any rules, orders or acts issued, promulgated or performed by public servants pursuant to decrees, orders, rules and regulations issued and promulgated by me or by my duly designated representative x x x"

What Rights remain after these?

1) Shutdown of, and imposition of government control over, all media and other means of giving out information;

2) Arrest and detention, in most cases without charges or complaint, of thousands allegedly involved, wittingly or unwittingly, in a conspiracy to overthrow the government.

3) Placing of all public utilities under military supervision;

4) Banning of mass action in rallies or demonstrations, of criticisms of public officials and of the inalienable right of workers to strike and picket.

5) Closing of all schools for one week. (Actually, it was a month. I remember)

6) Imposition of curfew from 12 o'clock midnight to 4 o'clock in the morning, reduced later to from 1 o'clock in the morning to 4 o'clock in the morning.

7) Carrying of firearms outside residence without the permission of the armed forces of the Philippines became punishable by death.

8) Suspension of the departure of Filipinos abroad, except on official mission.

The reason Martial Law was declared was because Democracy was starting to work as evidenced by protests borne out of the grievances by the poor and marginalized. These then put pressure on institutions that were designed to address such in the first place. That the pressure was applied because of better organizing and conveyance of messages that have long been unheard and ignored.

Marcos used this as a picture that Democracy was in danger from the same people who wanted to benefit from the fruits of a real and responsive democracy.

But what did constitute the consolidation of the powers of the Executive, the Legislative and the Judiciary upon one man by virtue of the declaration of Martial Law by Marcos? Marcos usurped the powers of bot co-equal branches of government by issuing the following:

General Orders. This was for the Armed Forces of the Philippines (AFP). In General Order No. 1 which was dated September 22, 1972, "NOW, THEREFORE, I, Ferdinand E. Marcos, President of the Philippines, by virtue of the powers vested in me by the Constitution as Commander-in- Chief of the Armed Forces of the Philippines, do hereby proclaim that I shall govern the nation and direct the operation of the entire Government, including all its agencies and instrumentalities, in my capacity and shall exercise all the powers and prerogatives appurtenant and incident to my position as such Commander-in-Chief of all the armed forces of the Philippines, x x x"

This enabled Marcos to control not just the Executive Department but also those that composed local government units who were under the Civil Service and also those appointed by elected officials.

Letters of Instructions. This enabled Marcos to control the entire civil bureaucracy regardless of the Security of Tenure afforded by the rules and regulations of the Civil Service Commission.

Also, Marcos specifically barred the Judiciary from vital areas of judicial functions, notable among which was any case involving the validity, legality or constitutionality of Proclamation No. 1081 (the Declaration of Martial Law) itself and "any rules, orders or acts issued, promulgated or performed" by him or his duly authorized representatives.

Marcos also created Military Commissions or Tribunals to try civilian cases. Also, Letter of Instructions No. 11 that gave Marcos the power to remove members of the Judiciary at will and even without cause.

Upon the declaration of Martial Law, Marcos issued a Letter of Instructions to all government personnel that they tender their resignations. They were considered fired if Marcos accepts their letter of resignation. Thus, Marcos controlled everything and all rights were abolished. It is a lie that there were rights that were retained.

Contreras said:

There is a need to diligently account for every death, pain and suffering during martial law, if only to give us an accurate picture of how much of it was done in the context of legitimate political warfare between the state and the CPP-NPA-NDF, and how much of it was done in excess of such and were blatant forms of unwarranted political violence.

It is too simplistic to give a blanket label to all these deaths as unwarranted atrocities. The death of an unarmed civilian mistaken to be a communist sympathizer is different from the death of a communist guerrilla who died while engaging military forces. The death of a captured sympathizer who resisted arrest and was involved in a gunfight with his captors should be distinguished from someone who was tortured and executed by paramilitary or government forces while in custody.

The pain and suffering of students who chose to take up arms should not be dismissed as insignificant. But these should not be seen in the same way we see the pain and suffering of their families who were even harassed by agents of the state as a consequence of their choices.

The narratives of pain and suffering during the period of martial law are so complex that it is total historical irresponsibility to lump all of these as exhibits for the evil which was conveniently simplified as a Marcos monopoly.

I say:

Of course there is a need to diligently account for all the sins of Marcos and Martial Law. But not in the context of those who suffered, died and were imprisoned was because of the political warfare between the CPP/NPA/NDF.

In the 1946 Nuremberg Trials, Goering, Hess, Speer, Doenitz, von Runstedt and all the other German generals and Nazi Ministers all pled not guilty. But they were sentenced nonetheless because history, the outcome of the war was enough evidence that they were wrong. Was the Nuremburg Tribunal wrong when it ruled and gave a blanket label to all the atrocities committed? No. It was the right thing to do. We have yet to have such a tribunal but history is the ultimate tribunal. Now, there are efforts to change the tribunal or orient it to an obscene direction that totally turns a blind eye to what transpired during those dark years. If the Martial Law era was so complex, then WWII was even more complex but they (the Nuremberg Tribunal) made the correct decisions not based on nitpicking. To point out that there are details (numbers of killed, imprisoned tortured because of actual combat operations) have not been hashed out and that until we have the details then Martial Law was not so bad after all is the height of intellectual dishonesty.

Contreras said:

Professor Ambeth Ocampo, a noted historian, has virtually thrown a challenge to all of us, when he revealed the state of mind of Ninoy Aquino who, according to declassified US documents, insinuated some level of support for Marcos' decision to declare martial law. Even more interesting, Ocampo also revealed how Ninoy even had the musings of a dictator himself, when he intimated that if he were President, he would execute all corrupt officials.

I say:

Prof. Ambeth Ocampo quoted declassified US documents. That is well and good. But there are also documented evidence that Aquino defied the declaration of the coming Martial Law. He made that expose in the senate with his privilege speech about Oplan Sagittarius, the blue print for Martial Law. Unknown to Aquino, there was indeed a blue print but the name of the blue print was based according to the sources that Marcos gave the plans. So "Sagittarius" was assigned to only 1 general and then Marcos knew who the leaker was. In spy novel parlance, the assignment of coded names to each recipient of any plan was called a "Canary Trap". The general was marginalized after that.

But getting back to Aquino, then Manila Mayor Antonio Villegas told Ninoy to flee the Philippines since according to his US Intelligence "contacts", Marcos is set to declare Martial Law anytime soon. "But if Marcos declares martial law, he will have to get me within the first few hours, or he will never get me at all," Aquino restated a line he had given two days earlier to interviewers Marita and Jorge. Marita and Jorge were reporters of the Daily Express, a daily broadsheet ran by the brother of Imelda Marcos, Kokoy Romualdez. It was published in Daily Express.

There are also stories of how Aquino was warned by Enrile, Tatad and Col. Gatan (who eventually arrested Aquino) 40 minutes before the arresting party was to arrive. But Aquino still continued with is meetings with Sen. Tolentino, Sen. Padilla and others at the Hilton. He would get a phone call and then he would turn pale but after that return to his usual self. There were 3 phone calls. Then he called fellow senator into a bathroom and told him that Marcos just declared Martial Law and he will be arrested. He was arrested after that in the Hilton Hotel.

So, these documented stories, from a Marcos newspaper at that has more weight than declassified US documents. But again, why did Aquino kept harking on Oplan Sagittarius if he was in favor of Martial Law? Why does the sun rise in the east?

Contreras said:

It is narratives like these that force us to treat historical revisionism not as a revolting endeavor, but in fact as the preferred mode for researching and writing history. It is in being ready to objectively inquire into Ninoy and Marcos, and martial law, that we will be fair to our history.

A history that is blinded by hate will prevent us from having a total grasp of the complex events in our past. Consequently, it will constrain the healing of our nation's wounds and allow the self-interest of political elites to profit from it.

I say:

Where in the statements I wrote advocate hate with regards to the treatment of history? What I wrote gives the facts of what transpired in an Unknown History. It does not foment violence and hatred. In fact my intention was to give information on what transpired during that time. There are still stories to be told, many of them in the Human Rights Victims Claims Board being processed right now.

I go back to what I learned from my grandfather. If there is injustice, then rage against it. But most importantly try to find a solution. If nothing can be done about it at the moment, then make sure it never happens again.

The whoosh of the cane being heard before hitting the legs, buttocks and back of my grandfather's playmate more than 100 years ago is just like what the Filipinos felt during the height of Martial Law. There is anger but never turn it into hate. By hating we are no better than Marcos and his evil cabal. Of course evil must be fought on the beaches, the mountains, jungle fastness, in every village, city, road and if need be from house to house. But it is not done because of hate, it is because there must be justice. A justice based on those who prefer to be human even though it is seen as a weakness by an enemy that is unfettered by morals.

The real justice is that the whoosh of the cane be never heard ever again.

---oOo---

7.

Subject: Re: Did Rizal retract?
By Pazogie

Posted by: pazogie <pazogie2003@yahoo.com>
Sent: Tuesday, January 17, 2017 9:44 PM

There was, Fred. But since the Church is a closed book when it comes to such issues, we can only guess. My guess has a lot to do with advancing its interest but it is not without rational basis.

All of Rizal's last acts were Church related, principally for its benefit but never forgetting that to get what it wanted Rizal had to be sufficiently convinced to go along. It had to act astutely with a lot of Christ's compassion, not of the evil Friars, in convincing Rizal to end his life with the blessings of the true Church for the good of all – himself, his family, the Church, people and country.

I believe the best negotiating instrument the Church had then was its assurance that Rizal will die innocent of the crime he was convicted and forgiven by the Almighty God of the Catholics who would be also the God of the Protestants and God of all believers and non-believers. **His innocence was at the forefront of his last concerns. He will have to die assured of that innocence.** {*An innocence which the powerful Church can help his people understand after his death [a possible trade-off, but unnecessary if Rizal was overwhelmed with humility] Kung mayroong trde-off na ganito, parang naisahan si Rizal.*}.

His last letter to Blumentritt, written a day before his death, serves to confirm this. There was nothing of import in it but his declaration of his innocence and a peaceful death. He wrote: "My dear Brother, when you receive this letter. I shall be dead by then. Tomorrow at seven, I shall be shot; *but I am innocent of the crime of rebellion. I am going to die with a tranquil conscience."*

Fred, the letter begs a question to the seeker and user of truth: *How did he realize and assure himself that he will have still a tranquil conscience when the bullets rip his body unto death?*

Would you agree, Fred, that,

Rizal was a man of hope, love, justice and peace, His extraordinary [heroic] aggressiveness towards sinners was due to his keen knowledge and disciplined acceptance of them as virtues to live by; He knew how they are violated and restored; He believed in forgiveness as the best means to assuage the pains of one's guilt of sinning; All those he may have been hurt by his acts for himself, family and country must be reached and forgiveness sought with offers of restitution whenever possible; All those who sinned against him must be forgiven; He has mastered humility and love because without them there is no sense in believing and doing forgiveness; Those who seek it are humbled and love fostered or restored;

All these were generously shown by his last acts. All done for tranquility sake - for him and all those around him, including those who knew him not, and for his country. All done leaving a great hope that everyone can move on towards each one's destiny - to the heaven of his own belief or design. All those who saw him walk his last steps witnessed a calm man [unafraid to face death and his maker, whoever it may be] and may have believed in his innocent. **His cool demeanor unchanged but courage bolstered as he saw in his mind his "audience, "including the dirty Friars, believing in his innocence.**

Now Fred, if this be Rizal's truths and by them alone, how would you judge him as a man, a Christian, a patriot and a hero?

All the best, *Ogie*

Did Rizal Retract
By Pazogie
From: pazogie <pazogie2003@yahoo.com>
Sent: Monday, January 16, 2017

Did Rizal retract? Sorry, but Yahoo mail did it again. It sent my unedited post inadvertently. Here's the completed edited message, Fred. Hi Fred, sorry if you feel a bit aggrieved by my "brilliant" reply. I take you as such and like to treat my friends as more than the ordinary man in the streets. Of course, it is a subjective assessment that may not be shared by you or our co-posters in the list. I appreciate your asking but you and I know there was more to it than an ordinary innocent curiosity.

I understood that well. EAAA Calderon sometimes needs assistance; we all do, in certain topics not of his expertise. I took his statement with a "help me attitude" as there was a reasonable gap in his arguments [culled directly from the horse's mouth but unsigned and unsupported] that he may have overlooked, which if assisted he may be enlightened or further be curious on how the truth of his "uncanny" conclusion may be supported, the truth uncovered, or in which direction it may be further pursued.

On a court's witness stand, what a witness says MAY JUST BE the truth. Who knows if he is lying? A dying [death bed] person's testimony to be of legal use can only be taken as a probable truth [he could be lying, too], not a stand-alone incontrovertible evidence that needs no corroboration from reliable witnesses. Besides, an Ode or a Farewell is not a clear and distinct testament of "Returning to the Catholic Fold". A testament will state the purpose, the name of the testifier [affiant], affix his signature, date, and bears the signatures of the witnesses. Rizal knew these requisites as it was required of his Manifesto and Retraction. If he was the author of the Ode and wished to be known, he knew well enough to put his signature and date. The fact that he didn't is evidence enough of ambiguity and makes for a lot of speculations of his true intentions and the authenticity of the contents. Thus, no one can truthfully say that the ode was also an admission that he went back to his old faith while "being manipulated' by the Friars to hurriedly signify to dubious "midnight attestations."

With Rizal's alleged last testaments [Manifesto, Defense, Retraction, Ode or Farewell, and "martyrdom"] I stand by my previous post assertion that IMHO Rizal had knowledge and probably wrote all of them BUT all done cautiously in good faith to protect the parties in interest, the best way he could under his present circumstances. Allow me to explain: 1. The controversial Manifesto: all the significant "evidence" point to a no direct participation in Boni's Katipunan. He was clear and consistent in asserting that a revolution at the time could not win on account of a poorly "educated" compatriots being misled into thinking they can win against a far more superior and a world power Spain; having been misled means, for one important consideration for the hero that the people should be spared from extreme retribution; Rizal by his actions in Spain and manifested desires in his letters only wanted reforms and was bidding for the right time, under the protection of Spain, later at the right time to ask for independence. It serves also Rizal in his failed defense.

The parties in interest here were: the Filipino people, Spain and Rizal;2. His "honest" Defense: The parties in interest, primarily was himself. If acquitted he will be given the opportunity to guide his people, first in their education, thence whatever it may take to take them towards independence; independence via a good relations with the world power Spain.

In his death, he was hopeful, that the winner of the revolution, Spain may be able to think along his way for a win-win solution;3. The contentious Retraction: Serves him best. He was hoping for a trade off or to reverse the authorities' Friar-infected-will to judge him guilty and shot to death. A freed Rizal was good for the Filipinos and Spain. In the process of reformation the Friars get to be benefited.

The untitled, undated, and unsigned Ode or Farewell: Sensing no other recourse but death, he tried to make peace with everyone, putting himself at ease and in peace while readying for his death; giving his family hope for a better life since he agreed to the Friar's wishes to cooperate; giving the people the message to rethink Boni's rebellion, to look his way - to educate themselves first, to critically think of his proposition for reforms, to endure and strive for a better partnership with Spain which will surely redound to Spain helping them gain independence. It should help appease the Friars, give them confidence that with his backing Boni's hopes of winning will dim and die in due time. The parties in interest in this instance are still the same - Rizal, the people and Spain.

His "unclear" martyrdom: A disloyal subject, a traitor, as nations decreed, must suffer the consequences of death. The death penalty serves as a warning to the rebels and would be sympathizers. It was done to help Spain regain its authority, win the war, assess its true economic and political interests in the archipelago, and while still owning a much valued trading post Filipinas, it proved an attractive bargaining chip to the Americans, during the Paris peace talk that served to diminish Spain's world prestige.

The Americans in a surprise twist of fate would become Rizal's protective big brothers, the vehicle towards our eventual independence. His assertion of innocence served his moral righteousness. Indeed, in my view, he was not disloyal even as he was very critical of the Friars and the local authorities of tyranny with impunity that mother Spain may not be aware of. Spain was forced to execute Rizal, not entirely because of the Friars "fixing" but mainly to preserve its dominion in RP, its naval power in the Far East, and its undquestioned ownership that proved a helpful "trading baggage" in its peace negotiation with the USA for self preservation, hoping to be able to stay a strong power, although diminishing as history proved. In my view, Rizal was working for his people, homeland, Spain and himself as he racked his brain for a win in what appeared to be a winless situation inside a secured jail.

He thought he found the only possible answer as his mind frenziedly moved along the romantic corridors where heroes and martyrs roamed towards their tragic destined end with a full audience applauding despite the gore and gloom they fostered by accident, innocence or with full consent. A person who gives his life in whatever way is a hero if done consciously with love for his family and homeland.

[Una persona que da su vida de la manera que es un héroe si hace conscientemente con amor por su familia y su patria/Ang taong nagbigay sa kanyang buhay sa kahit anong paraan ay isang bayani kung sadyang ginawa daladala ang lubos na pagmamahal sa kanyang pamilya at sariling bayan.]

Sa panahon noon, si Rizal ay maaaring ituring isang bayani dahil daw, wika nga, isang dakilang martyr. Itinuturing nga. Ngayon ganun pa din ba? Maaring yes, maraming sang-ayon nito. Ngunit, hindi kaya, dahil sa nangyari sa kanya na binaril na hindi sa kanyang kagustuhan hindi kawal ng rebelyon, maituturing isang civilian "collateral damage"lang siya? Hindi po ba? He was not a martyr because he was not a rebel or an active party to the rebellion. But he was in other ways a hero - charitably, understandably or even logically when he is to be considered "marked man" to be disposed at the opportune moment by the avenging evil Friars. It may be assumed, without fear of contradiction, that he died "heroically" for writing his anti-Church novels and secretly mapping a peaceful course of action for attaining reforms at the disadvantage of Spain, possibly disenfranchising and putting the Friars in shame at their rightful place; doing it for love of family, his people and country.

When Dr. Pio Valenzuela came to recruit him he rejected the offer, instead he gave good advices - of caution, to rethink the decision and not to proceed at the time, which Bonifacio, erroneously, took as an insult, an act contemptuous of his intelligence and honor as the Supremo; an act of disloyalty against the revolution. Thus, the forward looking Rizal, made good his heroism with a well contrived and sound reasoning in his 2nd stanza of his Ode or Farewell, which herein I quote,

"En campos de batalla, luchando con delirio, /Otros te dan sus vidas sin dudas, sin pesar; /El sitio nada importa, ciprés, laurel o lirio, /Cadalso o campo abierto, combate o cruel martirio, /Lo mismo es si lo piden la patria y el hogar."

That I translated into [without regard to poetry standards, mindful only of one paramount saving idea he wished to impart for his soul to completely rest in peace. Sa buong akala ko. Aaay. pasensiya....]:

"In the fields of battle, fighting deliriously, many give their. lives without doubts, regret [or profound reasons]; The place does not matter - cypress, laurel or lily, Scaffold or open field, [etc.] [Or, does the manner -] combat, cruel martyrdom, [or assassination, etc.] The same is true if done for the [love of one's] homeland." With due respect, Ogie Pssst...

I may have digressed from many translations. My fault. It is because I believe a last poem must leave the imprints of one's genius. It is different when others, even the best forgers, do it for him. [It is clear to me that the poem did not undergo a formal editing.] Rizal by his attempt to write his 3rd novel, Makamisa, understood very well the necessity of writing a farewell in his native tongue because this time he no longer was addressing his "Spain" but his "Patria" of native speakers. Also, I think no matter how much I try to translate, even if I happened to be the best poet, I could not translate a Spanish poem into English in toto, including everything [it is impossible for me to impart cultural emotive words and expressions in English from Spanish, Poor, poor me] that can best and only be done if one has been nurtured by the same tongue and only if one can walk himself through all Rizal have learned and experienced, knows his deepest secrets, have similar minds, thought processes and aspirations for himself, for all he loved - individuals , peoples and countries. I believe these translators are doing the impossible in making us fully understand Rizal's poem in English or Filipino.

Did Rizal Retract – My Rejoinder
Pazogie

From: pazogie <pazogie2003@yahoo.com>
Sent: January 15, 2017 8:06 AM
Subject: Re: [CebuPolitics]

Here's my rejoinder, Fred. EAAA: Most people I know and scholars told me that you .do not have to go to a third source to know whether our hero made the retraction or not. They said that in reading the stanza below written by our hero, you can have the truth from the proverbial expression "horse's mouth'. Rephrase d: I [Rizal] go to where God reigns, where there are no slaves, executioners or oppressors, where faith does not kill. Fred asked: Does the statement say Rizal returned to the Catholic Church? [Rephrased from the original: How does the above indicate retraction or non-retraction FROM THE CATHOLIC CHURCH?] ANALYSIS: Proposition from EddieAAA Premise 1: After retraction Rizal said, "I go to a Kingdom where there are no slaves, executioners, or oppressors; where faith does not kill. Premise 2: In that Kingdom reigns God. CONCLUSION: Thus, Rizal was going to the Kingdom of God. COMMENT: Our brilliant brother Fred knows better than to ask a question whose answer cannot be logical ascertained from the above vague proposition.

IMHO, the return to Catholicism issue is better evaluated and concluded from the DATED, SIGNED & WITNESSED RETRACTION statement of Rizal than from the UNDATED, UNSIGNED & UNWITNESSED and even UNTITLED Ode, dubbed inappropriately if not incorrectly as the Ultimo Adios. Retractionists will of course yell NOOO, the Ode is the better document because it was written by Rizal, smuggled out from prison hidden inside an alcohol stove [as claimed by his sisters who received the stove but didn't witness the writing] and by knowledgeable friends/technical individuals and handwriting experts that validated the Ode and invalidated the Retraction [but did no evaluation how the Original poem's paper would fit inside the stove, and no scientific evaluation of the paper and handwriting was ever done.] Both writings were alleged to have been made during the last days of his life in jail. Mere allegations without sufficient supporting evidence will lead us nowhere in satisfying Fred.

You know, it is important to consider Rizal's emotional state at the time of writing. Who can truly say or and prove that Rizal was serious and sincere in writing the Retraction? In writing every word/idea in the Ode? [As I have asserted in past posts, ONLY Rizal and God, if it exists would know for sure. Others can only come up with best guesses.] In the clear absence of sufficient facts the following Relevant Questions have to be asked but whose best answers may not necessarily redound to a clear conclusion of Rizal's Return to the Catholic fold dilemma:

1.   Did he sign the Retraction freely on his own volition without coercion or a trade off? How would we know the truth on this?

2.   Was he serious and sincere in writing the Ode? If he was why didn't he sign it to show that it really came from him? How do we know the truth on this, too?

3.   If the Ode was a genuine document from Rizal, why the secret sending/giving when the Ode's Godly reference and tone was in conformity [not contradictory] with the subject/text of the retraction and in EAAA's interpretation? Why be secretive with a very important document showing proof of his return to the Catholic fold, which effectively complemented/ corroborated the retraction? Thus, to send it secretly does not make sense. If he was the author, how will we know his true intention in sending it secretly unsigned? A good mind bender, eh? Giving him the benefit of the doubt says he had good reasons. So be it. Er, but give to Caesar what belongs to Caesar?

4.   If the Church wanted a genuine Retraction [with no neutral or pro-Rizal witnesses], won't the Church want a corroborating

document, such as an all important Adios, which was an imperative and can only be made in writing, not orally due to the very strict security measures of his confinement in jail?

5. If the Church deemed it a very compelling need, won't it be better to get it out through the proper channels via Rizal's grieving family and not to anyone else? Would it not be proper for the Church to get the Retraction and the Family - the corroborating Ode? Give to Caesar what belongs.....

6. If the Church manipulated both documents, would it be correct to conclude that both were genuine?

7. If the Church manipulated both documents, would it be correct to outright deny the retraction and the unsigned Ode?

DISCUSSION: Without any coercion, a manipulation of the Church may not necessarily affect the truth of the documents, including the Manifesto, does it? Rizal can play along so everyone gets a compromised agreement, for a compelling reason [of exigency or immediate necessity] agreeable to all parties. But the sincerity or the question of his truthfulness, without the sufficient substantiation will have to remain unsettled. Be that as it may, for the peculiar way I see the issue at this moment in time I can take both the Retraction and Ode [including the Manifesto] as genuine, i.e, done by Rizal, but remain doubtful of their sincerity. This step I take in great reverence to the man Rizal, sad, depressed, confused and needed, as he saw fit despite the hardship of his confinement and impending death, to act in the best interests of all concerned, particularly of his loved ones, his oppressed family, pathetic people and unheralded undeveloped neglected PATRIA [in its true meaning of HOMELAND at the time when. no Filipino nation existed yet; not the patria of most poem translators/interpreters. Bah!].

For all he has done, appreciated and unappreciated, to his people and his homeland, we are all wonderfully indebted, most especially for his nation building success formula for a fledgling nation to put itself first under the tutelage and protectorate of a great power before seeking independence! This to me was his greatest contribution, recognized, much appreciated and followed by the Americans that the innocent PDu30 hates so much]. Thus, I am compelled to give him, gladly with a warm heart and apologetic soul, the benefit of the doubt [without reservations, [smile] . May we all look at him kindly during our remembering and in our reflections do our best to seek out the best and worst in him for our guidance that we, he and us, may one day fulfill our common dreams for our PATRIA adorada, region del sol querida, perla del mar de oriente. With due respect to the great man, I would like to share this with you: when the uprising broke out, I was on board the Castilla, incommunicado, and I offered myself unconditionally to His Excellency, a thing that I had never done before, TO SUPPRESS THE REBELLION. I have always been OPPOSED to rebellion because I was hoping Spain would give us soon liberties, as I told Pio Valenzuela, because I could see that in order to forestall future events, A VERY CLOSE UNION BETWEEN SPAIN AND THE FILIPINO PEOPLE WAS NECESSARY. - Dr. Jose Rizal, Data for my defense, Fort Santiago, 12 December 1896 Have a nice day, all. Pit Senyor to all [most especially to home coming bro Martin] –

Ogie Pssst. Necessity knows no laws. Rizal in his last days of heroic martyrdom preparation [more intensely passionate than Jesus] knew this, was guided by it and applied it well. May the good man RIP. He had to be a pacifist until his last day. It was all his great mind allowed him to do. My sympathies. He knew perfectly well his time for bloody fighting didn't come yet and won't ever come, only for his misguided Boni and Agui captive people. [how unfortunate!]. Even at his martyrdom moment, he would only allow his own blood to be spilled. Thus, the order of a no rescue was made to his brother Paciano.

---oOo---

8.

Who is JPR

Marcelo Tecson
Posted: Tuesday, 17 January 2017,

I have further comments on Rizal, but here is just my quick reaction to herein forwarded email: A good general does not waste the lives of his soldiers in the face of certain defeat without any strategic purpose for the impending loss of the soldiers' lives -- they sue for peace or even surrender. World history is replete with this case, such as what Gen. Jonathan Wainright did in Bataan in WW II, and Gen. Charles Lee in the American civil war in the 1860s, and Japan in 1945.

But a better general would not even start a war if he would not win. Both Germany and Japan built up first their military power before starting WW II. They pick their battles, as in the case of Gen. Sam Houston while constantly retreating from the Mexican forces of Gen. Sta. Ana in the Texas revolution after the disastrous incident at the Alamo. Once the impatient Gen. Sta. Ana divided his forces into two groups to find the elusive Gen. Houston, the latter surprised and attacked one of the groups which included Gen. Sta. Ana and captured him.

In the case of Rizal, he was sure that the revolution would fail and would just duplicate past tragic rebellions, like the Cavite revolt that led to the martyrdom of Gomburza, the failed revolt of Diego Silang who was emboldened by the capture of Manila by the British during the time of Gen. Simon de Anda in the 1760s, and many other unfortunate incidents.

To begin with, we were not even a nation then in substance, and Bonifacio's cry of Balintawak -- which in the first place was merely provoked by the friars' discovery of the secret Katipunan society -- would have been just another rebellion had Gen. Aguinaldo's forces not been winning in Cavite, understandably not given as much Spanish attention and defense compared to Manila where Bonifacio did not win any battle. After the death of Bonifacio, the Spaniards concentrated on Aguinaldo and he began to suffer defeats in battles, leading to his continuing retreat to Bulacan until he SURRENDERED under the Pact of Biak na Bato in San Miguel, Bulacan, received some compensation from Spain, and was exiled with some of his key officers in Hong Kong.

Now, why should we find fault in Rizal if he did not want to be part of an untimely revolution, which he correctly foresaw as bound to fail?

---oOo---

9.

Premature Revolution & Rizal's Retraction

Roberto Bernardo
Posted: Jan. 17. 2017

I think M. Tecson's Jan. 9 post got it right, to quote him: "Rizal against PREMATURE revolution [of 1896]...[ending] in unnecessary bloodshed and failure... rightly or wrongly...(he was for doable) reforms...leading to opportunity for more education and enlightenment. ...resulting in turn to nationalism and readiness to govern....(much later) nationwide revolution if need be."

I think Ogie agrees judging from his earlier post from which I quote: "[in 1896] there was no Filipino nation YET to speak about....only thousands of separate islands...." Based on these historical facts, we're forced to admit that JPR died as a critical but liberal Spanish subject! As Ogie wrote: Hindi po ba binobobo natin si Rizal tuwing nagpupumilit tayo na ang loyalty niya ng panahon binaril siya ay sa Filipino Nation [na wala pa noon]"

Or that he's a great PH hero because he inspired, if not secretly directed, the glorious 1896 PH Revolution for PH Nationality and independence.   Note however this does not mean he was not a great martyred hero. On the contrary it took heroic courage to disown the Katipunan' s 1896 bloody adventure, to tell Bonifacio, thorugh Valenzuela, in effect: "Abort your fool's revolt!" But those two hid this from their fellow rebels and continued on with their failed uprising in Rizal's name. Binobo din nila yata si JPR, at ginamit lang siya sa recruitment at paglaban nila.

On Rizal's Retraction:

Just a minor point on the late Austin Coates whom I relate in one of my retraction-falsifying books I interviewed twice in the mid-1990s. Neither British envoy nor ambassador was he ever but served in Hong Kong as a magistrate. He moved on to research and write probably the finest biography of Rizal, probably equaled in quality by Carlos Quirino's unread pre-War classic. The former from start was completely anti-retractionist while the latter took a publicly neutral stance. The Rizal scholar, Pres. Quezon, rated the latter the best biography he had ever read, and I agree. It's even much better than the famous postwar ones by Joaquin and Guerrero, who didn't even know for sure why Rizal was the premier PH National Hero.

One of Coates' main disproofs of the Retraction is the retraction-falsifying December 30, 1896 Adios itself!. While the Jesuits claimed they spent practically the whole last day of the "29th-30th" with the condemned dying alleged rebel, persuading and guiding him through the writing and spiritual celebration of the signed retraction, especially from 11PM to 7:03 A.M. throughout the whole night in the death cell itself. In actual fact, Coates argued with the facts and other arguments, there was no such all-nightlong "sleep-in" by Fathers Balaguer and another named Jesuit whose name I used to know very well (as he was a favorite teacher of JPR in science and philosophy but now can't recall in old age). In fact, Coates argued, Rizal was alone during the night, rushing the final-finishing of the writing of the defiant Adios and arranging for its safe smuggling out, in the stove-lamp in the big pile of other keepsakes and personal items. He took pains to be allowed by the authorities to let Taviel de Andrade deliver it all in the hands of family representatives right after his death. And it was so done, Coates assured me from evidence he himself had gathered from his specially close relations with the main Rizal descendants, In my second interview, he even laughed out in that loud voice of his at the posturing Knights of Rizal's negligence in not making this clear to everyone.

---oOo---

10.

Rizal's Retraction:
A Note on the Debate
Rev. Dr. Eugene A. Hessel

(A lecture given at Silliman University, February 15, 1965. Dr. Eugene A Hessel was Professor of New Testament at Union Theological Seminary, Dasmarinas, Cavite.)

(When I was a young college student in the early 1950s, Rev. Dr. Hessel was the Administrative Pastor of Ellinwood-Malate Church. I knew him from the perspective of a young member of that church. This article is included in this book, with courtesy and permission of his surgeon-son, Dr. Eugene A. Hessel of Kentucky University Hospital. – Tatay Jobo Elizes)

This is a debate in which this lecturer hesitates to take part. For one thing, I believe there are aspects in the life and thought of Dr. Jose Rizal which are of far greater significance. I have already expressed this view In my book, The Religious Thought of Jose Rizal, (01) and I shall have more to say about it in the concluding part of this lecture. It is most unfortunate that some people speak and write about the Retraction without really knowing what Rizal did or did not retract, i.e., not sufficient attention has been given to the mature, quite uniform and systematic religious thought of Dr. Rizal. Only when this has been done first can one evaluate the meaningfulness of the Retraction. For some people to retract would mean little, for they have so little to retract. This was not so of Rizal, and I have tried to make this clear on my previous lectures and writing. It Is the life and thought of Rizal during his mature years which are of primary interest to me, and not what happened during the last day of his life.

Another reason I hesitate to enter the "debate" is that some of the protagonists have generated more heat than light. There has been a great deal of "argumentum ad hominem," i.e., vitriolic attacks upon opponents in the debate. I do not wish to engage in such. I have respect for a number of Roman Catholic defenders of the Retraction. I treasure a letter received recently from one who has written four books defending it. He says, after reading my book, "I wish to congratulate you for your ... impartial appraisal of the man [Dr. Rizal]." Father Manuel A. Gracia, the discoverer of the Retraction Document, has been most gracious in personally helping me with my research.

Recently, however, I have been looking into the question of the Retraction with some interest and I intend to continue my research. I find that there are four common attitudes toward the 'Retraction' and its bearing on the life and character of Dr. RIzal:

1.   There are those who insist that

the Rizal to be remembered and honored is the "converted" Rizal. This is the official Roman Catholic position. In the only "official" book dealing with all aspects of the Retraction ("official" in the sense that it bears the Imprimatur of Archbishop Santos), Rizal's Unfading Glory, Father Cavanna says in the Preface:

Rizal's glory as a scholar, as a poet, as a scientist, as a patriot, as a hero, may some day fade away, as all worldly glories, earlier or later do. But his glory of having found at the hour of his death what unfortunately he lost for a time, the Truth, the Way, and the Life, that will ever be his UNFADING GLORY. (02)

This same sentiment is echoed in the statement issued by the Catholic Welfare Organization In 1956 and signed by the Archbishop with regard to the Noli and the Fili:

... We have to imitate him [Rizal] precisely in what he did when he was about to crown the whole work of his life by sealing it with his blood; we ought to withdraw, as he courageously did in the hour of his supreme sacrifice, "whatever in his works, writings, publications, and conduct had been contrary to his status as a son of the Catholic Church."

2.   There are those who have argued that Rizal throughout his mature life was a "free thinker and unbeliever"; thus the Retraction is of necessity a lie. This is the extreme opposite of the Roman Catholic position. My previous writing has tried to demonstrate that the major premise on which this thesis is based is not true.

3.   A third implied view may be summarized as follows: the RIzal that matters is

the pre-Retraction Rizal; therefore one can ignore the Retraction. The fundamental assumption here is held by many students and admirers of Rizal, including myself, but the conclusion does not necessarily follow. This brings us to the fourth possible attitude towards the Retraction.

4.   Scholarly investigation of all facets of Rizal's life and thought is desirable. In the Interest of truth, the truth to which Rizal gave such passionate devotion, we have every right, and also an obligation, to seek to know the facts with regard to the Retraction. If scholarly research continues, fancy may yet become acknowledged fact.

Before we proceed further it would be well to say something about bibliography and method. More than twenty books and pamphlets, in addition to numerous articles have been surveyed in the course of this study. A number of writings on the Retraction merely repeat the arguments of earlier ones and add nothing new. Others are more sarcastic and sentimental than enlightening. But something of value has been gained from almost all of them. The literature belongs to two general categories: biography, and works dealing specifically with the Retraction. Among the biographers, Guerrero, (03) Laubach, (04) and Palma (05) have given the most adequate treatment of the Retraction, the first accepting it and the other two rejecting it. Of works dealing specifically with the Retraction, the most objective, scholarly and complete are those by Pascual, (06) arguing against the Retraction, and Father Cavanna (07) in its favor. As an almost complete compendium of information and arguments pro and con there is no book to date which is the equal of that of Father Cavanna. The second edition has 353 pages of text, appendices, and bibliographical entries totallng some 123 Items. (A new edition just off the press is enlarged further but could not be utilized, incidentally. Father Cavanna draws heavily upon the documents and information supplied by Father Manuel A. Garcia.) Amongst other writers consulted, special indebtedness to Collas, (08) Ricardo Garcia, (09) and Runes and Buenafe (10) should be mentioned. Garcia is a prolific popular writer in defense of the Retraction; the other two oppose it. All tend to chiefly summarize what has previously argued although Runes introduces several new arguments which will be examined in due course. Much research time has been spent in running down various versions of the Retraction Document appearing in books, articles, newspapers, etc. in writing letters to clarify or verify certain points, and in conferring with individuals. Unfortunately, many documents were destroyed during the war.

The story of the Retraction has been told and retold. Various newspaper reports of the last hours of Rizal were published on Dec. 30, 1896 or the days shortly thereafter. However, the first detailed account came out in a series of anonymous articles m the Barcelona magazine, "La Juventud," issues of January 15 and 31 and Feb. 14, 1897, republished some months later in a booklet entitled La Masonizacion de Filipinas — Rizal y su Obra. Some thirteen years later, Father Vicente Balaguer, SJ., the Jesuit priest who claimed to have secured Rizal's Retraction, asserted that this account was his work which he originally wrote "that very same night of

December 29, 1896. (11) Subsequently, on August 8, 1917, Father Balaguer repeated his story in a notarial act sworn to by him in Murcia. Spain. The only detailed account is that by Father Pio Pi y Vidal, S. J., Superior of the Jesuits in the Philippines in 1896, who published In Manila In 1909, La Muerte Cristiana del Doctor Rizal, and confirmed his account in a Notarial Act signed in Barcelona, April 7, 1917. In brief, the Jesuit account is this: On the 28th of December (the very day Governor General Polavieja ordered the death sentence) Archbishop Nozaleda commissioned the Jesuits to the spiritual care of Rizal, indicating that it would probably be necessary to demand a retraction and suggesting that both he and Father Pi would prepare "formulas." Thus, about 7:00 a.m. of the 29th, two of the Jesuits arrived at the temporary chapel where Rizal was to spend his last 24 hours. During this day various Jesuits came in and out together with other visitors, including members of his own family. Rizal also took time to write letters. Arguments with Rizal, with Father Balaguer taking the leading part, continued until dusk, by which time, according to the Father's account, (12) Rizal was already asking for the formula of retraction. That night Rizal wrote out a retraction based on the formula of Father Pi and signed it about 11:30 p.m. The Retraction contains two significant points: (1) the rejectton of Masonry ("I abominate Masonry") and (2) a repudiation of "anything in my words, writings, publications, and conduct that has been contrary to my character as a son of the Catholic Church. "together with the statement "I believe and profess what it teaches and I submit to what it demands." During the night there followed, according to the Jesuit accounts, several Confessions (some say five), several hearings of Mass, a number of devotional acts, the asking for and signing of devotional booklets intended for various members of his family, and finally at 6:00

a.m. or thereabouts, some fifteen minutes before he was marched out of Fort Santiago to his execution, a marriage ceremony was performed by Father Balaguer for Rizal and Josephine Bracken. So much for the story in outline. Details, including the text of the Retraction, will be presented and discussed later.

Before assessing the validity of the account a brief word should be said about the history of the controversy concerning the Retraction. One way to arrive quickly at an overall view of the course of the debate is to read the titles and dates of pamphlets and books dealing with the subject such as are contained in any good bibliography of Rizal. A seemingly accurate description of the history of the struggle in convenient form is found in Part II of Cavanna's book which reports the various attacks down to the publication in 1949 of Ozaeta's translation of Palma's biography of Rizal. Cavanna seeks to answer the various arguments against the Retraction, and in doing so makes reference to the chief works defending it. The first stage of the Debate lasted for some twelve years after Rizal's death, and at least overtly was wholly one-sided. Cavanna aptly calls this period on of "Concealed Attacks." The newspapers published the reports given to them presumably by the Jesuits. Within the first year the Jesuits published a quite complete story, for the time being anonymous in authorship. In successive years other books and booklets were devoted in whole or in part to repeating the same story, culminating in the famous full length biography in Spanish by Wenceslao Retana who incorporates the Jesuit account. Yet even in the early years of this first period there were a few small voices raised in objection, quite surprising since a totalitarian regime combining Church and State was in control. Cavanna himself lists a leaflet dated Manila, December 31, 1896 and several letters questioning the retraction. (13) Their main point, stated or implied, is that the Retraction is not in keeping with the character of Rizal. It is of interest that at the end of the period, just a year after the publication of his own biography of Rizal, Retana has something similar to say in an article dated Dec. 29, 1908. Although still not denying the retraction, he adds:

. . . The fact is that influenced by a series of phenomena, or what is the same, of abnormal circumstances, Rizal subscribed that document, which has been so much talked about, and which no one has seen ... The conversion of Rizal... was a romantic concession of the poet, it was not a meditated concession of the philosopher. (14)

We may accept Cavanna's dating of the second period as covering from 1908-1935. This is the time of vigorous open attacks, many of them by Masons. Ever since, somewhat unfortunately, an active battle has been waged between Roman Catholic and Masonic protagonists. Early in the period, m 1909 to be exact. Father Pi published his booklet La Muerte Cristiana del Doctor Rlzal.   This was answered three years later in a long article by Hermenegildo

Cruz in which several arguments often repeated subsequently were presented, chief of them being: Where Is the Retraction Document? The debate drew forth in 1920 the most serious Roman Catholic answer until recent times, namely Father Gonzalo Ma. Pinana's Murio el Doctor Rizal Cristianamente? Which Is chiefly significant because it reports a series of notarized accounts made in the years 1917-1918 by the chief "witnesses." The period seemingly closes with victory for the defenders of the Retraction, for after many challenges to show the actual Document of Retraction on May 18, 1935 it was "discovered" by Father Manuel A. Garcia, CM., while he was archdiocesan archivist was busily sorting through a pile of documents that they might be arranged in orderly fashion in their new fireproof vault. On June l6th the news was released by The Philippine Herald.

I would date the last period of the Debate from 1935 until the present. This is the time when, in the light of the Retraction Document discovery, major and minor works have been written on the subject of Rizal's life and thought as a whole and on the Retraction in particular. This leads us naturally to an assessment of the chief arguments pro and con which have been raised over the years and systematically dealt with in the last thirty years.

As one examines the issues brought forth in the debated, a tabulation of the chief ones raised since 1935 (the year of the discovery of the alleged Retraction Document) indicates that a sort of impasse has been reached. Similar points are now made over and over again. In what follows   I shall not devote myself to presenting detailed answers to detailed arguments. This has been done in book after book.

Furthermore, as any college debater or trial lawyer knows, it is possible to present an objection to almost any statement, and the effect so far as the audience is concerned is often the result of a subtle turn of phrase or an appeal to a bit of loyalty or sentiment. Rather, we shall be concerned with the thrust of certain main positions which taken individually and in their accumulative significance serve to swing the weight of unbiased conviction from one side to the other. Finally, we shall offer some suggestions for escaping from the present stalemated debate.

What, then, are the major arguments for the Retraction? Although the arguments had been presented by others before him, Father Cavanna gives a well organized summary which is adopted by most subsequent defenders. The points which follow are based on Cavanna with some minor modifications:

1.   Since the discovery in 1935, the Retraction "Document" is considered the chief witness to the reality of the Retraction, itself. In fact, since then, by words or implication, the defenders have said: "the burden of proof now rests with those who question the Retraction."

2.   The testimony of the press at the time of the 'event, of "eye-witnesses," and other "qualified witnesses," i.e. those closely associated with the events such as the head of the Jesuit order, the archbishop, etc.

3.   "Acts of Faith, Hope, and Charity" reportedly recited and signed by Dr. Rizal as attested by "witnesses" and a signed

Prayer Book. This is very strong testimony if true, for Rizal was giving assent to Roman Catholic teaching not in a general way as in the case of the Retraction statement but specifically to a number of beliefs which he had previously repudiated. According to the testimony of Father Balaguer, following the signing of the Retraction a prayer book was offered to Rizal. "He took the. prayer book, read slowly those acts, accepted them, took the pen and saying 'Credo' (I believe) he signed the acts with his name in the book itself." (16) What was it Rizal signed? It is worth quoting in detail the "Act of Faith."

I believe in God the Father, I believe in God the Son, I believe in God the Holy Ghost, Three distinct Persons, and only One True God. I believe that the Second Person of the Most Holy Trinity became Man, Taking flesh in the most pure womb of the Virgin Mary, suffered, died, arose again, ascended into Heaven, and that He will come to judge the living and the dead, to give glory to the just because they have kept his holy commandments, and eternal punishment to the wicked because they have not kept them. I believe that the true Body and Blood of Our Lord Jesus Christ are really present in the Most Holy Sacrament of the Altar. I believe that the Blessed and ever Virgin Mary, Mother of God, was in the first moment of her natural life conceived without the stain of original sin. I believe that the Roman Pontiff, Vicar of Jesus Christ, visible Head of the Church, is the Pastor and Teacher of all Christians; that he is infallible when he teaches doctrines of faith and morals to be observed by the universal Church, and that his definitions are in themselves binding and immutable; and I believe all that the Holy, Roman Catholic, and Apostolic Church believes and teaches, since God who can neither deceive nor be deceived, has so revealed it; and in this faith I wish to live and die.

The signed Prayer Book was amongst the documents discovered by Father Garcia along with the Retraction.

4.   Acts of Piety performed by Rizal during his last hours as testified to by "witnesses."

5.   His "Roman Catholic Marriage" to Josephine Bracken as attested to by "witnesses." There could be no marriage without a retraction.

These arguments are impressive. Many think of them, as Cavanna does, as "irrefutable facts. "But to call them "facts" is to prejudge the case or to misuse the word. That a Retraction Document was discovered in 1935 is probably a fact but that is a document actually prepared and signed by Rizal is the question at issue. As we shall soon see, many opponents of the Retraction use the Document as their chief argument. So also, there is a signed Prayer Book. But a number have asked, is this really Rizal's signature? Granted, for sake of argurnent, that it is, what is the significance of a mere signature apart from the testimony of Father Balaguer as to why Rizal signed?

What about the testimony of the "witnesses?" We may dismiss the newspaper reports as being less significant though of corroborative value. Their news was secured from others. One reporter got into the chapel during part-of the twenty-four hours. He states that "studies, frolics of infancy, and boys' stories, were the subject of our chat." (17) As for the actual eye witnesses, some eight testified to having seen one or more of the acts mentioned above. Only three testify to having seen the signing of the Retraction. The major witnesses are priests or government officials at a time when Church and State worked hand in hand. The bulk of the testimony comes from notarized statements in 1917 or later. Having made these remarks, it is none the less true that the testimony is impressive. It cannot be dismissed, as some have tried to do, with a few sarcastic comments. The argument from testimony as well as the arguments as a, whole can be better judged only after weighing this evidence over against the arguments rejecting the Retraction.

What is the case against the Retraction?

1.   The Retraction Document is said to be a forgery. As we have noted, the Document plays a significant part on both sides of the debate. There are four prongs to the case against the document itself.

a.   First of all there is the matter of the handwriting. To date the only detailed, scientific study leading to an attack upon the genuineness of the document is that made by Dr. Ricardo R. Pascual of the University of the Philippines shortly after the document was found, a study which he incorporated in his book, Rizal Beyond the Grave. Taking as his "standard" some half dozen unquestioned writings of Rizal dating from the last half of December 1896, he notes a number of variations with the handwriting of the Retraction Document, the following being the most significant ones according to the present lecturer:

(1) the slant of the letters in the standard writings gives averages several points higher than the average yielded by the Retraction Document, and perhaps more significantly, the most slanted letters are to be found in the Document;

(2)   there are significant variations in the way individual letters are formed;

(3)   with reference to the signature, Pascual notes no less than seven differences, one of the most significant being indications of "stops" which, says the critic, are most naturally explained by the fact that a forger might stop at certain points to determine what form to make next;

(4)   there are marked similarities in several respects between the body of the Retraction and the writing of all three signers, i.e. Rizal and the two witnesses, thus serving to point to Pascual's conclusion that this is a "one-man document."

The only scholarly answer to Pascual is that given by Dr. Jose I. Del Rosario as part of the thesis which he prepared for his doctorate in chemistry at the University of Sto. Thomas, 1937, although most of the details are the result of a later study which Father Cavanna asked him to specifically prepare. (18) Dr. del Rosario's main criticism may be said to be that Pascual does not include enough of Rizal's writings by way of comparison. On the basis of a larger selection of standards he is able to challenge number of Pascual's statements although this lecturer has noted mistakes in del Rosario's own data. Dr. del Rosario's conclusion is that the hand writing is genuine.

TEXT OF THE RETRACTION DOCUMENT DISCOVERED BY FATHER GARCIA IN 1935 IN THE ARCHIVES OF THE ARCHDIOCESE:

Me declare católico y en esta Religion en que nací y me eduqué quiero vivir y morir. Me retracto de todo corazón de cuanto en mis palabras, escritos, impresos y conducta ha habido contrarío á mi cualidad de hijo de la Inglesia Católica. Creo y profeso cuanto ella ensena y me someto á cuarto ella manda. Abomino de la Masonería, como enemiga que es de la Inglesia, y como sociedad prohibida por la Iglesia. Puede el Parelado Diocesano, como Autoridad Supeior Eclesiastica hacer pública esta manifestación espontánea mía para reparar el escándalo que mis actos hayan podido causar y para que Dios y los hombres me perdonen. José Rizal El Jefe del Piquete. El Ayudante uplaze Juan del Fresno Eloy Moure.

Based on a Photostat of the Retraction in the files of Rev. Manuel A. Garcia, C.M. seen by this lecturer. TEXT OF THE RETRACTION AS REPORTED BY FATHER BALAGUER IN HIS NOTARIAL ACT OF AUGUST 8, 1917

Me declare católico y en esta religión en que nací y me eduqué quiero vivir y morir. Me retracto de todo corazón de cuanto en mis palabras, escritos, impresos y conducta ha habido contrario a mi cualidad de hijo de la Inglesia. Creo y profeso cuanto ella enseña; y me someto á cuarto ella manda. Abomino de la

Masonería, como enemiga que es de la, Inglesia, y como Sociedad prohibida por la misma Iglesia. Puede el Parelado diocesano, como Autoridad superior eclesiástica, hacer pública esta manifestación, espontánea mía para reparar el escándalo que mis actos hayan podido

causar y para que Dios y los hombres me perdonen. Manila, 29 de Deciembre de:1896. Esta… retractación la firmaron con el Dr. Rizal, el Sr. Fresno Jefe del Piquete y el señor Moure, Ayudantede la:Plaza. Cf. Gonazlo Ma. Piñana, Murió el Doctor Rizal Cristianamente? (Barcelona: Editoríal Barcelonesa, S.A., 1920); p. 155

b. A second prong directed against the authenticity of the document itself is based on the principles of textual criticism, Several critics, beginning so far as I know with Pascual, have noted differences between the text of the document found in 1935 and other versions of the Retraction including the one issued by Father Balaguer. (19) Since this kind of criticism is related to my work in Biblical studies I am now engaged in a major textual study of .my own which consists first of all in gathering together all available forms of the text. To date, it is dear from my own studies that at last from the morning of December 30, 1896 there have been, discounting numerous minor variations, two distinct forms of the text with significant differences. The one form is represented by the Document discovered in 1935 and certain other early records of the Retraction. Two phrases in particular are to be noted: in line 6, "Iglesia Catolica," and in line 10 "la Iglesia." The other form of the text is much more common beginning with the text of Balaguer published in 1897. In place of "Iglesia Catolica" in line 6 there is the single word "Iglesia" and in place of "la Iglesia" there appears "la misma Iglesia." There also tend to be consistent differences between the two types of the text in the use of capital letters. The second form also claims to be a true representation of the original.

The usual explanation of these differences is that either Father Balaguer or Father Pi made errors in preparing a copy of the original and these have been transmitted from this earliest copy to others. Father Cavanna makes the ingenious suggestion that Father Balaguer made corrections in the "formula" which he supplied to Rizal according to the charges which he supplied to Rizal writing out his own, but he didn't accurately note them all. On the other hand, it would have seemed that the copy would have been carefully compared at the very moment or at some other early date before the "original" disappeared. It is not surprising that some have wondered if the Retraction Document was fabricated from the "wrong" version of a retraction statement issued by the religious authorities.

c.   A third argument against the genuineness of the Retraction Document which also applies to the Retraction itself is that its content is in part strangely worded, e.g. in the Catholic Religion "I wish to live and die," yet there was little time to live, and also Rizal's claim that his retraction was "spontaneous."

d.   Finally, there is the "confession" of "the forger." Only Runes has this story. He and his co-author report an interview with a certain

Antonio K. Abad who tells how on August 13, 1901 at a party at ancestral home in San Isidro, Nueva Ecija (when Abad was fifteen) a certain Roman Roque told how he was employed by the Friars earlier that same year to make several copies of a retraction document. The same Roque had been previously employed   by Colonel   Funston   to   forge the signature of the   revolutionary General Lacuna   on   the document which led to the capture of Aguinaldo. Runes also includes a letter dated November 10, 1936 from Lorenzo Ador Dionisio, former provincial secretary of Nueva Ecija, who was also present when Roque told his story and confirms it. (20)

On the basis of the above arguments taken as a whole it would seem that there is reasonable ground to at least question the Retraction Document.

(2) The second main line of   argument against the Retraction is the claim that other acts and facts do not fit well with the story of the Retraction. Those most often referred to by writers beginning with Hermengildo Cruz in 1912 are as follows:

a.   The document of Retraction was not made public in 1935. Even members of the family did not see it. It Was said to be "lost."

b.   No effort was made to save Rizal from the death penalty after his signing of the Retraction. The usual rebuttal is that Rizal's death was due to political factors and with this the religious authorities could not interfere.

c.   Rizal's burial was kept secret; he was buried outside the inner wall of the Paco cemetery; and the record of his burial was not placed on the page for entries of Dec. 30th but on a special page where at least one other admitted non-penitent is recorded (perhaps others, the evidence is conflicting). It Is asked by the defenders of the Retraction, how else could an executed felon be treated? Perhaps the ground outside the wall was sacred also or could have been specially consecrated. To top the rebuttal, Rizal's "Christian Burial Certificate" was discovered on May 18, 1935 in the very same file with the Retraction Document! The penmanship is admitted by all to be by an amanuensis. Whether the signature is genuine is open to question.

      d.   There is no marriage certificate or public record of the marriage of Rizal with Josephine Bracken. To say that these were not needed is not very convincing.

      e.   Finally, Rizal's hehavlor as a whole during his last days at Fort Santiago and during the last 24 hours in particular does not point to a conversion. Whether written during the last 24 hours or somewhat earlier, Rizal's Ultima Adios does not suggest any change in Rizal's thought. The letters which Rizal wrote during his last hours do not indicate conversion or even religious turmoil. In the evening Rizal's mother and sister Trinidad arrive and nothing is said to them about the Retraction although Father Balaguer claims that even in the afternoon Rizal's attitude was beginning to change and he was asking for the formula of retraction. It is all well and good to point out that all the above happened prior to the actual retraction. A question is still present in the minds of many.

      (3) The third chief line of argument against

the Retraction is that it is out of character. This argument has been more persistently and consistently presented than any other. Beginning with the anonymous leaflet of Dec. 31, 1896 it has been asserted or implied in every significant statement against the Retraction since that time. It has seemed to many, including the present lecturer, that the Retraction is not in keeping with the character and faith of Rizal as well as inconsistent with his previous declarations of religious thought.

First let us look at the character of the man. Rizal was mature. Anyone acquainted with the facts of his life knows that this is so. Thirty-five is not exactly young and Rizal was far more mature than the average at this age. It is not likely, then, that he would have been shocked into abnormal behavior by the threat of death. He had anticipated for some time that the authorities would destroy him, and even the priests admit that during most of his last 24 hours Rizal manifested a type of behavior consistent with all that was previously exhibited during his mature years. I worked closely with prisoners for some ten years and accompanied two of them to the scaffold. Their behavior was restrained and consistent. I would have expected Rizal's to be the same. Furthermore, in the deepest sense of the word Rizal was already a "believer." In my book and elsewhere I have argued strongly that Rizal was not a "free-thinker" in the usual sense of the word. History is full of the unchallenged reports of real conversions, but the most significant meaning of true conversion is the change from unbelief to belief, not mere change of ideas.

Rizal's conversion is also out of keeping with his mature religious thought. It is not as though Rizal had been bowled over by confrontation with the new thought of Europe (and by antagonism towards religious authorities who had injured his family and who worked hand-in-hand with a restrictive colonial regime) but had never fully thought through his religious convictions. As I have written elsewhere: "The fact that similar views are found from writing to writing of his mature years and that they made a quite consistent whole suggest that such theology as he had was fully his own..." (21) Rizal had a consistent and meaningful system of Christian thought, and it is therefore harder to think of his suddenly exchanging it for another.

So much for the debate up to the present. I have tried to state fairly the arguments, and it is perhaps evident on which side the lecturer stands. Nonetheless, I do not feel that the question is settled. What, then, remains to be done? Is there a way out of the impasse? Are there areas for further investigation?

(1)   Let a new effort be made to keep personalities and institutional loyalties out of future discussion. It is time for honest investigators to stop speaking of the "Protestant," the "Masonic," or the "Roman Catholic" view towards the Retraction. Let the facts speak for themselves.

(2)   Let the Retraction Document be subject to neutral, scientific analysis: This suggestion is not new, but in view of the present state of the debate and appropriate to the approaching 30th year since its discovery it would be fitting to at last carry this out. Furthermore, it

would be an act of good faith on the part of the Roman Catholic Hierarchy. If the document is genuine, those who favor the Retraction have nothing to lose; in either case the cause of Truth will gain. I would suggest for this analysis a government bureau of investigation in some neutral country such as Switzerland or Sweden.

Should neutral experts claim that the Document discovered in 1935 is a forgery this of itself would not prove that Rizal did not retract. But it would prompt further study.

(3)   As a third step, then, to be undertaken only after a new evaluation of the Retraction Document, the Roman Catholic Hierarchy should feel bound to allow its other "documents" pertaining to Rizal's case to be investigated, i.e. "the burial certificate," the signature of the Prayer Book, and perhaps also certain other retraction documents found in the same bundle with that of Dr. Rizal's.

(4)   The story concerning the "forger" should be investigated further.

(5)   If assurance can be given that the above steps are being undertaken then let there be a moratorium on further debate and greater attention given to the rest of Rizal's life and thought, in particular to his mature religious faith and thought. Let me close with the words of Senator Jose Diokno:

Surely whether Rizal died a Catholic or an apostate adds or detracts nothing from his greatness as a Filipino. It is because of what he did and what he was that we revere Rizal. . .

Catholic or Mason, Rizal is still Rizal: the hero who courted death "to prove to those who deny our patriotism that we know how to die for our duty and our beliefs" . . . (22)

(A lecture given at Silliman University, February 15, 1965. Dr. Eugene A Hessel is Professor of New Testament at Union Theological Seminary, Dasmarinas, Cavite.)

Bibliography:

(1)   Manila: Philippine Education Co., 1961.

(2)   Jesus Ma. Cavanna y Manso, C. M. Rizal's Unfading Glory, a Documentary History of the Conversion of Dr. Jos£ Rizal. 2nd. Ed. Rev. and Improved {Manila: n. n. 1956), p. vi. Subsequently referred ta'as "Cavanna."

(3)   .Leon Guerrero, The First Filipino (Manila: National bferoes* Com mission, 1963). Subsequently referred to as "Guerrero."

(4)   Frank C Laubach, Rizal: Man and Martyr (Manila: Community Publishers, 1963). Subsequently referred to as "Laubach."

(5)   Rafael Palma, The Pride of the Malay Race. Translated Roman Ozaeta. (New York: Prentice-Hall, Inc., 1949). Subsequently referred to as "Palma."

(6)   Ricardo R. Pascual, Rizal Beyond the Grave, Revised Edition (Manila: Luzon Publishing Corp., 1950). Subsequently referred to as "Pascual."

(7)   Jesus Ma. Cavanna y Manso, op cit. in footnote "1"

(8)   Juan Cotes, Rial's 'Retractions' (Manila: n.n. 1960). Mr. Collas was of great help in preparation of my book on Rizal's religious

thought. He handles both Spanish and English with consummate skill and has opened up to many English readers much of Rizal's thought by translating Rizal's most important minor writings.

(09) Ricardo P. Garcia, The Great Debate, The Rizal Retraction (Quezon City: R. P. Garcia Publishing Co., 1964). Subsequently referred to as "Garcia." Starting with a little booklet in 1960, this former school principal turned publisher has since published three enlargements of his original attempt to answer a number of works written against the Retraction, including those by Palma, Collas, Juan Nabong, Judge Garduno, and Runes using as his defense chiefly 1 Cavanna.

(10) IldefonsoT. Runes and Mamerto R. Buenafe, The Forgery of the Rial "Retraction" and Josephine's 'Autobiography' (Manila: BR Book Co., 1962). Subsequently referred to as "Runes."

(11) Cavanna, p. 24.

(12) Ibid, p. 8. Cavanna has conveniently included in his book most of the pertinent Jesuits accounts.

(13) Cavanna, pp. 144ff. — .

(14) Ibid, p. 153.

(15) Cavanna, pp. 1-108.

(16) Cavanna, p. 54. A Photostat of the Acts is found facing page 57 of Cavanna and the translated text on pp57f.

(17) Don Santiago Mataix, correspondent of the Horaldo deMadrid, quoted by Palma, p. 325.

(18) Cavanna, pp. 176ff.

(19) See accompanying page (inserted columns above) for the two "texts."

(20)   Runes, pp. 107ff. As a first check of my own on his evidence I wrote to a professor friend of mine whom I have known intimately for eighteen years. Since he comes from the North I thought he might be able to make some comments on the persons involved. To my surprise I found that my friend is himself a native of San Isidro, knew personally all three men mentioned above, and vouched strongly for their respectability and truthfulness. All had been civic officials. My informant had not heard the above story nor read the book by Runes, but he knows the   author personally and vouches for his "reliability and honesty."

(21)   Eugene A. Hessel, The Religious Thought of Jose' Rizal (Manila: Philippine Education Co., 1961), p. 255.

(22)   From the Preface to Garcia's The Great Debate. It is surprising and heartening that the senator would write this in a book defending the Retraction.

--ooo--

11.

Josephine Bracken Letter
Timeline, February 22, 1897

A direct transcription -- faithfully following errors of spelling and punctuation -- of a document reproduced as Appendix J in One Hundred Letters of Jose Rizal to his Parents, Brother, Sisters, Relatives (Manila: Philippine National Historical Society, 1959), 559 to 563.

(copied from internet for all to see. Tatay Jobo Elizes.)

Description Of My Life
22nd February 1897. Monday
My Mother is a Native of Ireland and was married to my Father on the 3rd of May 1868 In Belfast Ireland. My Fathers name is James Bracken, and my Mothers name was Elizabeth Jane Mac Bride. We were five brothers & sisters. Charles, Agness, Nelly, Francis, & myself Josephine. Charles was born on the 10th of April 1864. Agness was born in Malta on the 14th May 1873. Francis was born on the 2nd of June 1875 and died on the 1st September 1875. Nelly was born at Gibraltar on the 21st July 1871. and I was born in HongKong at the Victoria Barracks on the 9th of August 1876. My Father is a Corporal and Detachment Schoolmaster of a Detachment at Pembroke Camp. My Mother died on the 2nd of September 1876 after giving birth to me. After the loss of my beloved Mother I was then removed

to the care of a neighbor until after her burial. As my Father is a Military he could not attend to all of us especially me for being so very small he gave me to a family to be adopted. The kind benevolent Couple Mr. and Mrs. Taufer took very good care of me until I was seven years old. Unfortunately at that age was when my adopted Mother died.

This is When I was Seven Years of Age. 1882 Mrs. Taufer died on the 8th of October 1882 with a heart disease. A year after Mr Taufer took to another wife, then my troubles commenced little by little. On the 13th of July 1889 we took a trip up to Japan on account of Mrs. Taufers illness, we stayed in Japan three months but as her health did not recover we returned back to HongKong. We arrived in Hong Kong on the 24th of November 1889. But Mrs. Taufer got worse and died on the 26th April 1890.

This is when I was Fifteen years of Age. 1890. On the 12th November 1891 Mr. Taufer took to a third wife which was a torment to me. On the 12th December I left Mr. Taufers house and went to the Italian Convent because I could not stand any more her troubles. I stayed in the Convent two Months when Mr. Taufer came begging me to go home because his wife was starving him. As I could not hear him complaining I went back on the 3 February 1892 to take care of his house. On the 14th September I had trouble again with Mrs. Taufer and hunted her out of the house. In 1893 Mr. Taufer got very ill and had sore eyes, as he tried several Doctors but none could do him any good.

This was when I were Eighteen Years of age. On the 6th of September we went to

Manila for the purpose of seeing Dr. Jose Rie-zal. unfortunately Dr. Rie-zal was not in Manila but up the Provinces. We stayed in Manila for six Months and then we went up to Dr. Rie-zal place. We arrived in Dapee-tan That is the name of the Province on the 14th of March 1894 in the morning at 7 o,clock. We stayed their a week before Dr. Rie-zal operated on his eyes. After a weeks time Mr. Taufer could see a little. On the 22nd February Dr. Rie-zal asked Mr. Taufer if he had any objection if he marry me. But Mister Taufer objected it, but as I had affection towards Mr. Riezal I intended to marry him. I accompanied Mr. Taufer back to Manila and returned to Dapee-tan in the next steamer. By that time Dr. Rie-zal prepared every thing for our marriage, when everything was prepared I heard from a Spaniard that when we are married they would separate me from my husband. I thought it over and told Dr. Rie- zal that it is better for us to wait until he gets his freedom. anyhow I stayed with him for one year, and we lived very very happy. Thank God I had a very peaceful life as if I were a child on its Mother knee. I cannot complain of his care. Ha! yes but it did not last very long. My happiness lasted only 28 months then my sorrows commenced again.

This is when I was Nineteen years of age. 1896. On the 28th of July 1896 Dr. Rie-zal left Dapee-tan for Cuba as a Doctor in the army. But unfortunately they brought him back again and shot him on the 30th December 1896. before his execution he married me at 5 o clock in the morning.

This is when I am Twenty Years of age 1896. Josephine Bracken de Rie-zal, A Widow.

12.

Graceful Closure to MoveOn
Electoral College petition drive
A Remarkable Journey: *Reflections of a MoveOn Petitioner*

Michael Baer
Dateline, Early January 2017
(Duly acknowledging with gratitude and attribution to Michael Baer for this well-defined political article. The spirit of electoral college petition drive should go on in the near future.)

Eight weeks ago, Donald Trump was elected president of the United States. The MoveOn petition that I had authored on a lazy afternoon in the summer of 2012 suddenly came roaring into significance. It gained a half million signatures to abolish the Electoral College (EC), in the first six days after the election.

I knew that such a petition, no matter how many signatures it received, would not be easily translated into successfully ending the EC. Since the Bill of Rights was approved in 1791, only 17 amendments have been successful, and only two in the last 55 years. A supermajority of two-thirds of each house of Congress is required, and then it must be ratified within 7 years by three-fourths of all the various states. That means 34 Senators, or 13 states can block any amendment. I also learned that attempts to get rid of the EC has been tried numerous times. The greatest number of failed attempts to amend the constitution is this anachronism from our foundational document.

These are challenging obstacles under any circumstance. The framers intended it to be that way. But we live in a particularly polarizing era, and the candidate of the minority has just been awarded the keys to the kingdom. His base is mobilized. To abolish the college under these circumstances would be about as easy as breaking into Fort Knox using a biodegradable spoon and a toothbrush.

But back in mid-November, with the momentum of 500,000 fresh signatures, it still felt possible, and worthy of my best effort. The strategy quickly formed to develop a Facebook (FB) Community Page to create "views" and "likes" to drive new people to signing the petition, and to use the increasing popularity of the page to try to win celebrity endorsements of one kind or another. The FB page would act as a forum for conversations, brainstorming, sharing of information and dialogs as an attempt to create a community "brain" capable of meeting the challenges, while simultaneously trusting that opportunities would present themselves for meaningful action as the story unfolded. Build it… and the path forward will emerge.

What emerged was an engaging drama. Trump chose unconventional (and often frightening) cabinet appointments. He engaged in twitter conflicts with China, Saturday Night Live, the Press, and others. We learned more about Russian hacking. Jill Stein raised $7 million in four days to investigate voting anomalies in Midwestern mid-sized swing states. Those state courts shut her down, but not before she exposed serious voter suppression activity, and legitimate suspicions of outright voter fraud. A group calling themselves the Hamilton Electors raised the specter that electors had a duty to vote their conscience; country over party. Although it was an admitted longshot we watched with interest to see if the effort might flip the outcome or present the House with a compromise Republican alternative to Trump or Clinton. Our FB page reported all of it and more, posting three to five times daily on the various threads and stories, and in the process grew a following currently at 21,700.

Then, on December 19, the Electoral College endorsed Trump as anticipated with very few defections. We had imagined that such an outcome might create a backlash that could boost the petition drive further with another mighty wave of activity, perhaps pushing it over a million signatures. But in fact, the opposite happened. Signatures dropped from a range of fifteen hundred to three thousand per day down to a couple hundred per day and activity continues to wane. In the two weeks since the electors cast their ballots we have gained less than 2000 signatures. Granted it is the holidays, but it feels like the tide is out for a while.

Another eye-opening part of this journey has been participating in the community conversation of the FB page via the comments section available below each posting. I began by advising the community to ignore the "Trump trolls" i.e., the hateful, rude, obnoxious, and childish commenters whose strategies are reducible to expletives, insults, untruths, and gloating, often invoking all four in a mere sentence.

Over time I ignored my own advice and began trying to engage the trolls. I thought I might disarm them by asking sincere questions or injecting chiding humor without overtly insulting them as an effort to draw them into civilized discussion. Sometimes it worked and I felt minor victories when the troll became a human beneath the façade. We still disagreed, but a bridge of respect had been established.

But there is a constant influx of new trolls to the FB page, as we strive to expand the reach by doing some FB advertising to people who identify as interested in politics, government and voting, which brings in all stripes. Encountering all that negativity begins to feel like toxic psychological warfare, and the dreck starts to stick. After being provoked several dozen times, I began to feel the need to strike back; to "go low" with them. I have begun to do that, but what I hope is in a clever way.

That is a bit of a detour from the MoveOn petition drive, and I realize it is not helping the cause, nor is it healthy for me. I have become polarized, and in turn polarizing to others. This was not my intent when I started. It's time to drain my own swamp.

Eight weeks, and the way forward has not emerged. However, my views on the Electoral College have evolved during the journey. I used to think it was just old and antiquated, never updated because of a few special interests in a former era, and that these interests might now be overwhelmed by popular sentiment, motivated by recent results, and organized into the tip of a spear to cut through the antiquated and unpopular ideas.

Now I see it as something far more nefarious. It arose as a compromise to slave states during the founding of our union. It remains a powerful tool in the toolbox of the white supremacist minority. Combined with voter suppression techniques now exacerbated by the Supreme Court's decision to gut the 1965 Voting Rights Act, our voting system is deeply corrupted. Donald Trump was right about that: The system is rigged.

Many of you are aware of an alternative approach to neutralize the EC without amending the Constitution. It is called the National Popular Vote Interstate Compact (NPVIC) or more commonly, the National Popular Vote movement. Briefly, the idea is to develop a consortium or compact of states that agree (through their respective legislatures) to cast all their electoral votes for the national popular vote winner. This year that would have been Hilary Clinton. Once the consortium reaches critical mass attaining the majority of the electors (270 at the current time), then the compact becomes binding.

The strategy is very clever. As long as every state member sticks to the agreement it will have the desired outcome: the overall popular vote winner will assume the oval office. Currently the strategy is 61% of the way to its goal with 165 electoral votes in the compact. Notably, none of the consortium is from a traditionally Republican state.

To my mind, this noble end does not justify the means, which are egregious. If a state like Wyoming was in the compact this year and the compact was in effect, Wyoming would cast all their electoral votes for Clinton even though 80% of their voters chose Trump at the ballot box. That would understandably upset, and more importantly disenfranchise, an awful lot of Wyoming folk. Additionally, besides the potential for many states to individually reverse the will of their constituents, there is also a collective injury to all the states who do not join the compact. Here they are, playing by the rules created centuries ago, and a compact of other states just gave them the collective finger. We are already divided and polarized to a point where "civil war" has begun to enter the collective lexicon. I believe the NPVIC is a matchlight that can ignite the fuse to our doom, if it ever comes to fruition, which is itself a longshot.

So now what? If a constitutional amendment is impossible in the current climate, and the NPVIC is untenable and divisive, where does that leave us? I have come around to the idea of supporting Electoral College reform which does not require two-thirds of the congress and three-fourths of the states to agree. In fact, it is possible that only 5 people could decide to implement it as the law of the land.

The reform proposal would be to eliminate the winner-take-all aspect from the Electoral College. That protocol appears nowhere in the Constitution (nor does the idea of two party system for that matter). Winner-take-all evolved through the states' rules setting process for choosing electors over the years. The method by which elimination of winner-take-all in the states could be enacted is through the Supreme Court. The argument is that winner-take-all is a violation of the 14th amendment, the equal protection clause.

It is a compromise because several small states will still maintain their substantial per person voting power advantage over voters in larger states. But it means that every vote will count, because states' electors will be allocated based on the proportion of the popular will of the election. This year, California would break 35-20 for Clinton, and Michigan would have split 8-8. From reports I have read, the overall outcome would have been 270-263 for Clinton, with 5 electors being allocated to 3rd party candidates. The margin is quite close to the 2.1% popular vote margin.

The arguments for this proportional reform to the EC have been made by people far more scholarly and versed in Constitutional law than I, who is but an interested layman on both counts.

On January 3, 2017, the 115th Congress was sworn in, with each member taking a solemn oath to preserve, protect and defend the Constitution from all enemies, foreign and domestic. Never has the need to stand up for that oath been more essential in my lifetime... nor perhaps in my country's lifetime. I made my own oath shortly after election day to stick with this journey at least until now, so that the petition with 616,221 signatures and counting, could be delivered to the members of the new Congress. They will be sorted by the signers' zip codes, so that each petition will be electronically delivered to each signatory's House member and two Senators and President Obama.

I want to thank each, and every one of you, who were catalysts encouraging me forward each step along the path of this eight-week journey. Many of you sent me invaluable letters of kindness and encouragement or thoughtful strategies on how to proceed. I have learned valuable lessons; about social media, about the Electoral College, about my fellow Americans and about my own nature.

The petition drive is over, but the movement continues. I was a young boy during the revolutionary times of the 1960s and early 70s. But as I reached adulthood and looked back, I marveled that people literally stopped an unjust war, won civil and voting rights for Black Americans and other dispossessed groups, and began the environmental movement. It happened because a large enough group of average working citizens took time from their busy lives and stood up and said, "ENOUGH!

Our government and our culture has gone astray. We will not allow this to continue and just stand idly by, waiting for someone else to do something."

Fifty years later, I believe we are at a similar crossroads. Will enough of us collectively stand up and say "Enough!" The Electoral College is just one battlefield of injustice. History has shown that the American spirit can rise to the challenge. But will we? The answer is up to each of us to do what we can, to persist, and to realize that small things can become big things if enough of us take part. I believe it can be done... must be done non-violently despite the hate, anger and division we see in the polity. What does it take to make a Trump troll? We need to dig for those answers and diligently endeavor to find ways to include them in our collective solutions.

With deep gratitude, and hope tempered with foreboding.

Michael Baer MoveOn Abolish the College petitioner (Acknowledgement and Attribution to this well-defined article. Thanks.)

---oOo---

13.

The Killing Time: Inside Philippine President Rodrigo Duterte's War on Drugs
by anywhereiwander

Dateline: About Aug. 2016
(Posted by Jude Tagaciudad in Visayans Yahoogroup, as our Acknowledgement and Attribution to this important article).

Dondi   Tawatao—Getty ImagesRelatives weep as the coffin of an alleged thief and drug pusher, who was a victim of an extrajudicial killing, is laid to rest on Aug. 21, 2016, in Manila. As the body count soars, some say the real threat to the Philippines is not drugs but the President himself. At around 11 p.m. on July 25, Restituto Castro received an anonymous text message asking him to leave his house in the Caloocan district of northern Manila and come to the corner of the McArthur Highway. Just hours earlier, the Philippines' new President, 71-year-old Rodrigo Duterte, had given his inaugural State of the Nation address, in which he repeated the vow that saw him elected by a landslide in early May. "We will not stop until the last drug lord … and the last pusher have surrendered or are put either behind bars or below the ground, if they so wish," said Duterte. Castro, 46 and a father of four, was neither a drug lord nor a pusher. He never even bought grams of shabu — one of the local names for methamphetamine — for himself. Too poor to become a proper user —shabu starts at $31 a gram — he used to buy the drug on behalf of his friends in exchange for a bump or two. "He always had a hard time saying no to his friends," his wife Merlyn tells TIME. At the same time, a flirtation with meth didn't sit well with his life as a family man and his work as a chauffeur at a nearby hotel, and Castro decided to stop cadging recreational hits before he became dependent. According to his cousin, Castro told them that his next drug run would be his last. And so it was. A single bullet to the back of his head that night made Castro one of the first of nearly 2,000 Filipinos killed so far in Duterte's brutal war on drugs. The director general of the Philippine National Police (PNP), Ronald dela Rosa, told a Senate hearing on Aug. 22 that 712 people had been killed in police operations in the seven weeks since the crackdown began, and that another 1,067 had died at the hands of vigilantes. By one account, there is official pride in the death toll. Nobody can claim to be surprised. The carnage is exactly what Duterte promised. "All of you who are into drugs, you sons of bitches, I will really kill you," he said before his election, in April. A month later, when he was President-elect, Duterte offered medals and cash rewards for citizens that shot dealers dead. "Do your duty, and if in the process you kill 1,000 persons because you were doing your duty, I will protect you," he told police officers on July 1, the day after his inauguration. He was speaking at a ceremony installing dela Rosa, his loyal henchman, as the nation's top cop. "If you know of any addicts, go ahead and kill them yourself as getting their parents to do it would be too painful," he was quoted as saying to another crowd that day. And so the killing time began. The Philippines is hardly alone. Executing people for drug-related offenses, judicially or otherwise, is characteristic of the region. According to a report last year by drug policy NGO Harm Reduction International, the only countries other than Iran and Saudi Arabia known to have executed drug traffickers since 2010 are all Asian: China, Malaysia, Vietnam, Singapore and Indonesia.Thailand conducted its own war on drugs in 2003 under then Prime Minister Thaksin Shinawatra, and the events then — more than 13,000 arrests, over 36,000 cases of people surrendering to police, and nearly 1,200 deaths in its first month — will feel eerily familiar to Filipinos. Two decades earlier, a wave of extrajudicial executions took place in Indonesia under its autocratic leader Suharto. They came to be known as the petrus killings after the Indonesian acronym for penembak misterius (mysterious gunmen) and had as their supposed aim a reduction in crime. Thousands were murdered in the period between 1983 and 1985. Now, it's the Philippines' turn, and Duterte's war may turn out to be the most ferocious yet. "This fight against drugs will continue to the last day of my term," he said. That day is six years away. Noel Celis—AFP/Getty Images Jennilyn Olayres, center, cries as she follows the hearse carrying the coffin of her partner Michael Siaron during his burial at a cemetery in Manila on Aug. 3, 2016. Siaron was killed by suspected vigilantes on July 22 acting on President Rodrigo Duterte's call to kill all the country's alleged drug dealers "I don't care about human rights, believe me" Duterte got elected because he promised to be tough on crime. But how bad is crime in the Philippines, and is reducing it worth the summary massacre that is now taking place? The Philippines is not listed in all columns of this U.N. Office on Drugs and Crime (UNODC) survey of global reported crimes from 2003 to '14. But comparisons can be made using figures from a 2015 report issued by the Philippine Statistics Authority. There were 232,685 cases of crimes against persons involving physical injury reported in the Philippines in 2014, for a population of 98 million. By comparison, the UNODC says there were, in the same year, nearly 375,000 cases of assault in the U.K., which, with a population of 64 million, has far fewer people. In 2014, there were 10,294 reported cases of rape in the Philippines. But there were more than 30,000 cases in the U.K.; 12,157 in France (which has a roughly similar population to the U.K. at 66 million); and 6,294 in Sweden, for a population of just 9.5 million. That same year, there were 52,798 reported robbery cases in the Philippines. That's about as many as there were in Costa Rica (52,126 cases) but Costa Rica, with 4.7 million people, has less than a 20th of the population of the Philippines, so the Philippine rate is much lower. The total is also far fewer than the 171,686 cases reported in Belgium (population 11.2 million). Neither is firearm ownership high in the Philippines. According to theUniversity of Sydney's School of Public Health, which researches the number of privately owned firearms worldwide, there are 4.7 guns per 100,000 people in the Philippines, putting it at a lowly 105th place in a list of 179 countries. Finland has 45.3 guns per 100,000 people, Canada has 30, and Australia has 15. Unsurprisingly, while the Philippines can be a deadly place, it is not especially so. According to World Bank data, the Philippine rate of 9 intentional homicides per 100,000 people in 2013 makes it only slightly more dangerous than Lithuania (7) or Mongolia (7), and puts it on a par with Russia (9). The U.S. figure is 4. In the five years from 2010 to '15, PNP figures show that total murders across the nation's top 15 cities averaged 1,202 a year. But many more people have already died in the first seven weeks of Duterte's drug war. When Duterte made the eradication of crime the cornerstone of his campaign — pledging to kill "100,000 criminals" — he earned an emphatic victory, bagging 38% of the vote in a five-candidate race. This despite a demagogic boorishness that places him alongside some of history's most notorious rulers. On the campaign trail, Duterte's "joke" that he "should have been first" in the 1989 rape of an Australian missionary in Davao, and his public branding of his daughter as a "drama queen" after she revealed that she had been raped, were seen as salty stump speeches instead of indications of an ungoverned mind. His boast of the "1,700" suspected criminals killed by death squads during his time as mayor of Davao, where he was in office for 22 years, was also glossed over. (In April, he said that he would pardon himself "for the crime of multiple murder" if voted into the nation's highest office.) After his election, he has behaved just as bizarrely, making humiliating public references to a journalist's wife's genitals, and calling U.S. ambassador Philip Goldberg a "gay son of a whore." All of this has been overlooked, because Duterte is thought to be business-friendly and because, above all, he has promised to clean up the streets. But even allowing for the obvious caveats — like the fact that many crimes go unreported — it is clear from official data that the Philippines is not experiencing the sort of critical social breakdown that would explain an average of 36 extrajudicial killings a day. It could also be that Duterte wasn't really talking about pickpockets, or thieves, or carjackers, when he vowed to make "the fish grow fat" on the bodies he would dump in Manila Bay. He seems, in hindsight, to have been referring to only one kind of criminal: the drug users and drug pushers (many of them small time) that are merely the latest scapegoat of a nation that has long faced far greater problems, like endemic corruption, poverty, poor health, rights abuses, and a deeply entrenched culture of official impunity. Duterte once vowed to kill his own children, if he caught them using drugs. Now he sanctions the killing of other people's children, on the grounds that drug use is unforgivable moral laxity, robbing men and women of their rectitude, and the country of its silver. The overlords of the Philippine drug trade, he claims, are all in China — the ultimate destination, allegedly, of the grubby funds that furtively change hands on street corners across the land. But how bad is the Philippine drug problem? According to UNODC data, the highest ever recorded figure for the prevalence of amphetamine use (expressed as a percentage of the population aged 15 to 64) in the Philippines is 2.35. That is a high figure, but then the equivalent figure for the U.S. is 2.20, and the world's real amphetamine crisis is among Australian males, where the prevalence is 2.90. When it comes to illicit opioid use, the Philippine prevalence rate is just 0.05, compared to 5.41 in the U.S., and 3.30 in Australia. For cocaine, the Philippine figure is only 0.03. In the U.K., it is 2.40, in Australia 2.10 and in the U.S. also 2.10. Reuters Staff—ReutersA drug addict uses a glass water pipe to smoke shabu, or methamphetamine, at an undisclosed drug den in Manila on June 20, 2016

In other words, the statistics show what any visitor to the country may easily see: Filipinos are not degenerates, who need to be protected from themselves, but are mostly a nation of decent, sober, law-abiding and God-fearing people. The most revealing Philippine statistic is this: 37% of Filipinos attend church on a weekly basis. Less than 20% of Americans do. Nonetheless, Duterte has succeeded in convincing large numbers of his people that drug use constitutes such an emergency that the very existence of the nation is threatened, and that only his rule can save the Philippines. It's the oldest autocratic trick in the book. "We're on a slippery slope towards tyranny," Philippine Senator Leila de Lima tells TIME.A week after he took office, a poll conducted by Philippine research firm Pulse Asia showed that an astonishing 91% of Filipinos had a "high degree of trust" in Duterte. Among them are people like Ray Antonio Nadiera, a 33-year-old maintenance worker in the country's second largest city Cebu, who says that by the time Duterte's campaign is over, "all the addicts will be straightened out." In Manila's Pasig Line district, local resident Jamie Co says, "The people killed are the dirt of society. What Duterte's doing, his war on illegal drugs, is right. It's good."

"In the opinion of many Filipinos, law and order is a major issue and previous administrations weren't effective or dedicated in addressing it," Richard Javad Heydarian, a professor of political science at Manila's De La Salle University, tells TIME in an email. Duterte, he says, "has a lot of political capital to dispense with." But that was before the bodies began to pile up. Now, less than two months later, many others are appalled at the forces that have been unleashed. There is also deep shock at the drug war's financial implications: Duterte has given huge funding boosts to the police and military by slashing the country's health budget by 25%, and reducing expenditure on critical sectors like agriculture, labor, employment and foreign affairs. On the other hand, the budget for the presidential office has increased tenfold, and now includes a provision of $150 million for "representation and entertainment." "Whether it's state-sanctioned or not, I would say at the very least all of these killings are state-inspired," says de Lima. A former chairperson of the country's Commission on Human Rights and Secretary of Justice under the previous administration, de Lima has been waging an effectively lone battle from within the government against Duterte for the past two months.The 56-year-old lawmaker, who also heads the Senate's Committee on Justice and Human Rights, called for a probe into the extrajudicial killings two weeks after Duterte assumed office. She faced an intense backlash on social media from Duterte supporters, who vilified her as "a coddler and a protector," in her words, of the country's drug syndicates. Duterte's own response has been to launch a smear campaign; he is attempting to convince Filipinos that de Lima is in the pay of drug gangs and that she has had "sex escapades" (his words) with her driver, who, he suggests, collects bribes on her behalf. In the present climate, when people accused of far less are being shot dead, bandying around these sorts of tall stories is deeply threatening. Several colleagues in the Senate have also pushed back, dismissing an investigation as premature. "What's the threshold? Shall we wait for a thousand to be killed, or 10,000 or 100,000, before doing something?" de Lima asked TIME on Aug. 8, not imagining, presumably, that just two weeks later the first of those body counts would have been exceeded by almost 100%. Her sentiment is echoed by the international human-rights community. In June, two U.N. representatives condemned Duterte's "incitement to violence," not only against drug dealers and criminals but also against journalists. Duterte's response was "F-ck you, U.N." More recently, he called the international body "very stupid" for criticizing his war on drugs and subsequently threatened to pull his country out of it, despite the many programs run by U.N. agencies in the Philippines. He has also threatened to impose martial law. "This is going to damage democracy and the rule of law as we know it," says a Philippines-based international human-rights campaigner, requesting anonymity due to safety concerns. "This notion that you can solve all your problems just by killing people will only have a detrimental effect in the long run." Global advocacy groups like Human Rights Watch and Amnesty International have also denounced the slaughter and called on Duterte to change both his rhetoric and his policies. It's all the same to Asia's newest strongman. "I don't care about human rights, believe me," he says. "There is no due process in my mouth" As always, it is the poor in the barangays — as the smallest units of municipal organization are called — who pay the highest price. In these impoverished communities, barefoot children play beside open sewers, families often share a single room, and, for a few people, shabu is an escape — both psychotropically and financially. "A lot of the people involved in the drug market have no other opportunity for income, so a lot of that money also goes to support families in communities," says Clarke Jones, a researcher at the Australian

National University who has spent the past six years studying the Philippine prison system and the drug trade within it. "It's easy money," a 50-year-old detainee in Davao tells TIME. He says he's in jail for the second time after serving a drug sentence between 2003 and '08. "Sometimes you can't blame ordinary people who sell drugs because they do it to feed their families. It's just survival instinct." At this level, the effects of Duterte's war can be seen in the families left sobbing on the bloodied pavements. Families like that of Ricky Alabon.Alabon, 45, was gunned down on the night of Aug. 5 in the barangay of Malabon in northwestern Manila. He worked as the caretaker of his neighborhood's cell-phone tower and had gone to check on it around 11 p.m. According to a witness — a young child who relayed the incident to Alabon's younger brother Richard — he was surrounded by four men on three motorcycles, one of whom opened fire. Police found the father of four with 11 bullets in his body. "It's really savage how they killed him. The people who gunned him down are animals," Richard tells TIME, adding that his brother had gone clean weeks ago, after he saw his name on a list of alleged drug users being waved around by barangay leaders. "It's O.K. to eradicate drugs, what I don't like is the killings because there's still time for a person to change, right?" he says. "My brother, he actually changed." For the Alabon family, like many of the victims, seeking justice is out of the question. "We can't. We're poor," Richard adds. "What about his kids? They can't even continue their studies. How can we give him justice?" The second of those kids, 20-year-old Maricar, struggles to hold back tears as she tries to make sense of her father's death. "At the start of Duterte's time, it was happy because you could feel the change, but as time goes on, the trust is slowly fading," she says. "The police are supposed to help you, but they're the reason many people are dying." The assessment of Alabon's older brother George is more damning. "The government of Duterte? It's like Saddam, bin Laden, Gaddafi," he says angrily. "Hitler equals Duterte." Dondi Tawatao—Getty ImagesPolice examine the body of an alleged drug dealer and victim of a summary execution on July 14, 2016, in Manila In Manila's south, Jenny, a young woman, stands in a crowd of about 50 people, surrounding her neighbor's house at 2 a.m. on a Saturday. Gunshots were heard just over an hour ago, and the police emerge to announce that the occupant, a man named John Paul, has been killed. "It's like a death penalty is handed out without due process — Duterte gave free rein to the police," she tells TIME on the curbside. "They say if suspects fight back they can kill them, but people are getting killed without a fight." The police, on their part, claim that all their killings have been carried out in self-defense. And they have the unequivocal support of the country's new ruler, who has promised to "die" for them as long as they do their "duty." "This is the first time that the President and the administration are really focused on eradicating illegal drugs," says a senior police official, requesting anonymity. "The whole support of the President," he says, "makes it very encouraging for the law enforcer." The man leading the charge, 54-year-old PNP chief dela Rosa, has been Duterte's enforcer since the latter's Davao days. "Bato," as he is commonly known, was the southern city's police chief for more than a year, while Duterte was its mayor, and is known for his unflinching loyalty (in fact, he was sacked from the leadership of a PNP special unit in May, for making a pro-Duterte Facebook post a week before the election). "We maintain our trust and confidence in each other," dela Rosa tells TIME about his relationship with Duterte. He also rejects any suggestion that his officers are acting in any way outside the law, which he describes as a set of "constraints" that "we can deal with," before adding: "In the absence of evidence that proves my men are abusing, I maintain that they're maintaining regularity in the performance of their duties." That appears very conscientious given his closeness to Duterte, who is openly against the rule of law, despite being the son of a lawyer and a former Davao city prosecutor himself. "There is no due process in my mouth," the President said on Aug. 7. That night, he named 159 judges, public officials, and even police officers, whom he claimed were involved in the country's narcotics trade. He ordered that the policemen on the list be immediately dismissed, the politicians have their government-assigned security details revoked, and the judges to report to the Supreme Court within 24 hours. In the manner of a dictator, he chose to do this on live national television, naming one high-profile individual after another without providing any evidence. He may as well have been dressed in military fatigues of his own design. Erik de Castro—Reuters Philippine President Rodrigo Duterte gestures at soldiers during a visit at Capinpin military camp in Tanay, in the Philippine province of Rizal, on Aug. 24, 2016 "I'm trying to understand what this naming-and-shaming approach intends to achieve," says Jose Luis Martin Gascon, chairman of the Philippines' Commission on Human Rights. "He's angry at crime, so he's taking on the persona of everyone who's been victimized by crime?" Gascon adds: "The other problem, of course, is that when you do a naming and shaming in the current environment, you place these persons at potential risk of attacks from vigilantes. These are human beings, they've been accused, and they find themselves now in a gutter with a bullet in their head." The list itself is also full of mistakes. The country's Chief Justice, Maria Lourdes Sereno, pointed out in an open letter to Duterte that only four of the seven judges named were still on the bench. One of them was dismissed in 2007, and another died eight years ago. When she instructed that nobody named should surrender unless an appropriate arrest warrant had been issued, Duterte said that she "must be joking," and threatened to withdraw all executive support from her. Naturally, many of those named are appalled to find themselves accused of involvement in drugs — among them former Cebu mayor Michael Rama. "It really saddened us, we were shocked," Rama tells TIME at his family home in the city where he served as mayor from 2010 until May 2016, and as vice mayor for the decade before then. The 61-year-old veteran politician says he has always been against drugs, and cites a tripling of antidrug operations during his mayoral tenure as evidence. Rama believes that he was named as part of a settling of political scores, and cites "skirmishes from a long time ago" with Tomas Osmeña, the man who both preceded and succeeded him as mayor, that have "carried over." Rama is outwardly calm, but veers from making sycophantic remarks about the man who put him on the list ("We wholly support the relentless drive of this present administration, and I congratulate the President") to expressions of despair ("Right now I feel I am dead, even if I am alive"), to uttering constant invocations for the safety of his family. "I will never stop on behalf of the family," he says. "Not me. I can face it alone. I've had my struggles. But my primary focus now: get my family off this list." He may or may not succeed, but at least he has been able to fly to Manila and the dreaded headquarters of the Philippine Drug Enforcement Agency and secure an audience. That is a luxury that the country's poor do not have. "People here get really afraid now if they see anyone on a motorcycle wearing a helmet," a pastor in Cebu tells TIME, also requesting anonymity out of fear. His brother — one of four men gunned down by two attackers on Aug. 6 — was a drug user, but the pastor is struggling to make sense of his murder. "Why weren't they arrested? Why directly kill? It's bizarre, there's no due process," he laments. "This is a time of lawlessness." Ezra Acayan—ReutersLocal residents transport the bodies of two men reportedly killed in a drug raid in Manila on Aug. 18, 2016 "We don't have to convince anybody anymore"

Extrajudicial killings are not new in the Philippines. Historian Alfred McCoy — the author of several books on modern Philippine history — calculates that 3,257 people were killed by the regime of dictator Ferdinand Marcos, who ruled from 1965 to '86, while around 70,000 were imprisoned. (Duterte has openly expressed admiration for Marcos, and his decision to bury the former dictator at the Heroes' Cemetery in Manila led to the first public protests since the former Davao mayor took office.) Summary executions have not been unknown in the post-Marcos era either, particularly in the insurgency-ridden south. But the numbers have been low — an Asia Foundation report says that 390 people were killed in the 10 years to 2011 — until now. "Extrajudicial killings are a legacy from that authoritarian period," says Gascon, who was a member of the body processing reparations for the Marcos regime's victims before he became head of the human-rights commission last year. "But what makes it a little more difficult is that in previous administrations, postmartial law, it was not policy to support or encourage this kind of practice." Rightly fearing for their lives, Filipinos are surrendering in droves. More than half a million people have turned themselves in to the authorities for drug-related offenses, according to police data, since Duterte took office. Although, as Joseph Franco, an expert on the Philippines at Singapore's Nanyang Technological University, tells TIME via email, "Surrender is a very loaded term." The police draw up lists of suspected drug users and dealers, he explains. The lists are then sent to the barangay, where community leaders are pressured to endorse them and include additional names — something done with little verification or oversight, if any. "So you can put on those lists neighbors with whom you have an ax to grind" without worrying about a detailed vetting process, Franco adds. In this way, the poor are turned on each other. Once named, an alleged drug user has three options. To risk being murdered, to wait to be picked up in a potentially lethal police action, or to report to the authorities. If they choose the latter, they are made to sign a waiver saying they will swear off illegal substances — or face the consequences if they begin using drugs again. Erik de Castro—Reuters Residents of Makati in central Manila wait to take a pledge that they will not use or sell shabu, or methamphetamine, again after surrendering to police and government officials on Aug. 18, 2016 There are private rehab facilities, but most are full. The Bridges of Hope facility, for example, has room for just 92 patients divided between its two Manila branches. Its $650 monthly fee is well beyond the means of the average Filipino, who earns less than half that amount, but those that can afford it are flocking to its doors. "We now have to create a waiting list of some sort, which we didn't have to do before," says Guillermo Gomez, a program director. Since May 9 this year — the day Duterte got elected — he estimates there have been 500 inquiries from drug users or their families, an average of six a day. Before then, he says, the center received about three inquiries a week. "Lately, when the families inquire, we don't have to explain the program," he adds. "The decision happens so fast. We don't have to convince anybody anymore." Filipinos surrendering to the authorities, but unable to afford or get a place in private rehab, are often placed in community rehabilitation programs, where they can go to Zumba classes, or are taught trades like hairdressing or soap making. They also undergo weekly "value formation" sessions that serve as a barometer of their sincerity. "If these people will no longer attend [the sessions], it means they are already on the other side of the mountains, so we will be again running after them," says Jemar Modequillo, the chief of police in the city of Las Piñas, which is part of the Manila conurbation. "And those who are no longer interested to continue in this program, maybe that could be another story for them," he adds cryptically. Besides rehab, or the grave, the other destination for drug users is prison, which, even by the standards of the Philippines, is a special kind of hell. On a visit to Las Piñas City Jail, TIME estimated that about 50 men were sharing a roughly 10-by-10-sq.-ft. cell. Many had been there for over a month. But unbearable overcrowding is not unique to Las Piñas. With thousands of arrests over the past seven weeks, prisons around the country are overflowing. "Even prior to President Duterte's assumption of office there was a steady increase in the number of convicts admitted, but no increase in the facilities," says Resurrection Morales, who coordinates, on behalf of the Philippines Bureau of Corrections, efforts to reform inmates. The bureau runs seven facilities across the country that collectively house over 41,000 prisoners, which means they are already well past their tipping point, at 158% overcapacity. Noel Celis—AFP/Getty Images. This picture taken on July 21, 2016, shows inmates sleeping inside the Quezon City jail in Manila. Philippine officials said on Aug. 9, 2016, the government would build new jails to address severe congestion made worse by President Rodrigo Duterte's drug war, describing conditions as "inhumane" and "unacceptable" The maximum-security facility at Manila's New Bilibid Prison, where Morales met TIME, currently houses 14,000 inmates in cells designed to house no more than 6,000. Ironically, this is the place — not the poor and shabby barangays — from which the much of the Philippine drug trade is conducted. Duterte's administration is aware of this. The current Justice Secretary, Vitaliano Aguirre II, estimated in June that 75% of the country's drug deals could be traced back to New Bilibid. And yet, while drug users and low-ranking dealers are murdered outside the maximum-security compound, many of the country's top drug criminals lead lives of relative comfort and